THIS IS LONDON, GOOD EVENING

EDO LONDINO, KALISPERA SAS

© **Efstathiadis Group 2003**

ISBN: 960-226-606-6

EFSTATHIADIS GROUP **S.A.**
88 Drakontos Str.,
104 42 Athens
tel.: ++3210 5154 650,
fax: ++3210 5154 657
e-mail: efgroup@otenet.gr
GREECE

Printed and bound in Greece

George Angeloglou

THIS IS LONDON, GOOD EVENING

EDO LONDINO, KALISPERA SAS

The story
of the **Greek** Section
of the **B.B.C**
1939 - 1957

To Soteris Soteriadis

CONTENTS

George Angeloglou ran the Greek Section of the B.B.C. from 1939 to 1957

Author's Introduction

EDO LONDINO, KALISPERA SAS

«Edo Londino, Kalispera Sas». This is a short title for an eventful book, which covers some twenty years of life in the Greek Section of the BBC from 1939 to 1957. My life with the BBC started in August 1939 when the Corporation decided to enlarge its foreign services; adding the Greek Section to the German, French, Italian and Arabic services.

The narrative is on the lines of a diary that I kept assiduously during the first five years of the war and then again later, far less assiduously, for a number of years until I left Bush House in the summer of 1957.

I was fortunate to be given the opportunity to create a team which achieved excellent broadcasting standards all through the extremely difficult periods of Greek and international history. I wish to pay special tribute to the original group consisting of four young men and two young women. They came into Broadcasting House rather timidly, with little knowledge of radio, news and bulletins, but in a few months they became the Greek voices of courage, determination and hope. The original six, who worked with me, were Sotiris Soteriadis, Dino Gregoriadis, Vassilis Constantinidis and Anthony Mitsidis, and the two young women Mary Moschona and Kali Jenks. Throughout my time as head of the Greek Section I had an English secretary, Phyllis Reekie, who remained with me until I left Bush House.

George Angeloglou, 2001

George Angeloglou died on 3rd November 2001 before finally completing this manuscript. The final editing has been done by members of his family, who would like to thank Angela Rapps for her help with the original typescript.

Christopher Angeloglou, 2002

CHAPTER 1

THIS IS LONDON - EDO LONDINO
KALISPERA SAS

This is London, Good evening.

How can these four words, spoken in Greek from London many times a day, have sustained and encouraged the Greek people during some very dark days of the twentieth century?

And yet these words, spoken into a London microphone, did give strength, courage and hope to the Greek people during some three years when they were occupied by Italian and German forces.

It took quite a few months for the Greek Section - which originally consisted of only four young men and two young women - to find its feet. It was just as well because Britain, at the time, was not ready for war with Nazi Germany, after the period that had seen Neville Chamberlain and his followers come to power.

We, the small Greek Section, had to learn that we were reporting not on one, but on several fronts, which could change direction without warning. All these different events often imposed on us physical and mental stresses, which were often beyond our capabilities, but which never succeeded in breaking our morale. Four periods were particularly testing. The first was the collapse of France, the second was the nights of the Blitz on London in 1940-1, and the third later in the war, shortly after the Allied invasion of Normandy in June 1944, was the period of the flying bombs. Finally, and particularly difficult for us was the disastrous Greek Civil War which affected us all, and those who contributed to our broadcasts.

We drew inspiration from the great speeches of Winston Churchill, like the one he gave on the 4th June 1940. He threateningly advanced towards the dispatch box in the House of Commons to bellow at Hitler, "We shall fight on the beaches, in the fields, in the streets and in the hills. We shall never surrender!" That was a warning that Hitler took seriously!

In the pages that follow, I try to recall various important and often tragic events and let you make the acquaintance of many colourful individuals who often gave special meaning to our routine lives. Please read on and I hope you will be able to visualise what life was really like in our small Greek world in London between the eventful years of 1939 and 1957.

THE BEGINNING

It was 5.30 a.m., Tuesday, 3rd September 1940. The announcer and I walked down the corridor of the third floor of Broadcasting House to the front of the building where the Assistant Director General's office was located. He no longer used it as it had been converted into a studio like so many other VIP offices. It was a large, pleasant room with double windows, which had been curtained off with blinds made of special anti-acoustic material. It had a beautiful solid oak table covered with green baize with two microphones and two censor keys, one to each microphone. The censor keys were used if you wanted to cut off a transmission in order to talk to the announcer or, in an emergency, if you wished to interrupt a transmission for some reason.

As an adornment, the studio had a number of pictures on its walls, one of which was a large photograph of the first Director General of the BBC, Sir John Reith, the dour authoritarian Scottish Presbyterian who crea-

ted the independent public service BBC. To me it seemed as if the portrait of Sir John Reith was put there
with an ulterior motive; to prevent anyone from trying
to pass a message to the enemy, but also to stop any
hanky-panky taking place in the studio! I thought that
the grim look on the craggy face of Sir John was
enough to stop any erotic interplay between a producer
and secretary.

On that early morning, with central heating full on
and with no air conditioning, the studio was suffocating.
No announcer could stay fully awake for more than half
an hour in that atmosphere. Soteriadis immediately
complained "For God's sake, are we going to be asphy-
xiated tonight in these ghastly surroundings with the
D.G. looking down on us." I noticed that Soteriadis was
perspiring profusely and was beginning to look pale. So
very silently I got up and walked gently to one of the
nearest windows. I pulled the curtain back and managed to open both the inside and outside window. I felt
thoroughly satisfied with my efforts but completely forgot that the air raid alert was still on. The alert that
night had started at 7 pm but as no enemy planes came
over London, everyone forgot that there was an alert on.
As I went back to the table, the studio red light came on
and Soteriadis started reading the news. His voice
now was steadier and he looked cooler. Everything
was going to schedule.

Damage to the office in Broadcasting House

Suddenly, a few minutes later, the all clear sounded and the piercing wail of the air raid siren stormed into the studio. I went ashen. I rushed up and very gently closed the open windows while to my horror I heard

Soteriadis saying to Greece, "Dear listeners. That was the all-clear sounding in London after an all night alert. Now you know what a London alert sounds like...." I immediately pressed the censor key, which of course cut the transmission and shouted, "Are you mad, what the hell are you doing? You know this means big trouble. Broadcasting an alert or an all clear is strictly forbidden." Soteriadis just smiled and said, "But this is a broadcasting scoop. It's never been done before"... and then went on reading the news as if nothing had happened.

Two minutes later, the studio door opened and the duty officer and two security officers in uniform burst into the studio. I hushed them and they stood side by side in silence like three Spanish inquisitors until we had finished our broadcast to Greece. Then the uproar started. We were spoken to harshly, mocked and threatened. Enemy agents? The Tower? The sack? Actually, none of these things happened. We told the truth and the truth was accepted - followed by a strong reprimand. We had got off lightly. I felt relieved, but Soteriadis was blissfully happy. After all, he got his broadcasting scoop! And, by the way, a week later when I went into this same studio, I noticed that the austere Puritan, Lord Reith had a distinct subtle smile on his face. I don't think that smile had been there on Tuesday morning.

This alarming, yet amusing, episode in the history of the Greek Section happened just over a year after its creation. The BBC Greek Section made its first broadcast at 7.30 pm on the 28th September 1939; that is twenty-five days after the broadcast of Neville Chamberlain's fateful words "consequently, this country is at war with Germany".

I was recruited on the 10th September 1939 at a salary of £389 a year and found myself in charge of a Greek section consisting of six people - four young Greek men and two women. I was only 25, with no knowledge of broadcasting, and with a mother tongue which had not been in constant use since I had left my home in Cairo eight years before. At Oxford, where I read Law, I had met only one other Greek and later, during my studies for the English Bar, I had spoken Greek only with my guardian, Sir John Stavridis, and his family or when I went to the Greek Cathedral in Moscow Road.

So although by education I was well qualified for the job, my knowledge of the Greek language and Greek affairs was somewhat sketchy. Therefore, at the very start of my new profession, I felt somewhat insecure in the midst of a group of people, all of whom had been educated in the Greek language, and one of whom was a correspondent for two Athens newspapers. But the pressures and dangers of war and the good nature of all my staff made the early days with the BBC pleasurable and exciting.

21

Bunkbeds for the staff in B.H.

One of my colleagues especially, Sotiris Soteriadis, realising my weaknesses, went out of his way to be helpful. I owe him a great deal because it was largely thanks to him that I found my feet within a few weeks of my appointment as head of the Greek Section. Soteriadis, the most spirited and mature of the three announcers, was in fact the only experienced journalist in the section, except perhaps for the younger Anthony Mitsidis. Soteriadis was a gifted writer and commentator and for a number of years he wrote most of our political commentaries. Although born in Patras, he had more of the fiery temperament of a Maniatis, with a great caustic sense of humour.

Equally friendly and helpful were the other four members of the Section. They were: Dino Gregoriadis who was born in Constantinople of a northern Epirote family, and educated at the two excellent Greek schools of Constantinople, Zographios and Robertios. After studying law in Athens, he got a three-year scholarship to London where he did a Post Graduate degree in Economics at the LSE.

Basil Constantinidis was another Constantinopolitan but born of a Samiot father. His education was similar to Gregory's except he went into business when he came to London. Basil was a financial wizard and he did very well importing Portuguese sardines for the British government during and after the War. He was a quiet, sensitive, rather serious man who loved classical music. He had recently married an Athenian girl who shared his passion for music and their flat always echoed to the strains of Mozart, Chopin or Puccini.

Anthony Mitsidis, the youngest of the four men, came from Cyprus and represented the Nicosia newspaper, Eleftheria. Mitsidis was very exact in his grammar and often corrected mistakes in other people's scripts and reports. He was also a very competent typist both in Greek and English. But because of his Cypriot accent we did not use him that often as an announcer, as in those days the Cypriot accent was not approved of by Athens Radio.

And lastly, our very able secretary, Maria Moschona, at the time the only woman in the Greek section. Maria came from an intellectual family. She was the granddaughter of Souris and had inherited some of the gifts of her brilliant grandfather, who wrote and published an entire newspaper in verse. Her messages to us were always written in rhyming couplets and she also had the awful habit of shortening all our names to three or four letters. For example, Soteriadis was Sot; Gregory was Greg, Constantinidis was Con, Mitsidis was Mitsi or Misty and worst of all I was Angi. But you couldn't get angry with Maria, who was always calm and composed. Even during the worst air raids, Maria showed no fear. She went on typing regardless of bombs. The only fear Maria really had was of sexually active men. The only time I saw her disturbed and confused - for three days she didn't turn up for work, which for Maria was a sin, was when a member of the Swedish section made a pass at her in a taxi. After that, Maria never went in a taxi and never talked to any of our Scandinavian colleagues. The entire Greek Section adored Maria and she in turn looked after all of us with the concern and devotion of a mother.

CHAPTER 3

BROADCASTING HOUSE

We were, of course, delighted and very impressed that the Greek Section had been given an office in Broadcasting House, the famous headquarters of the BBC, in Portland Place, London W.1. BH, as it was endearingly called, was built in 1931, a magnificent white stone, ferro-concrete building which at the time was considered a revolutionary piece of architecture. The wide front of the building was semi-circular and a series of flat vertical planes rose sheer from the ground to six floors, then like the deck of a ship receded a little and went up two more floors. From a distance, this majestic white building resembled a large passenger liner about to sail down Regent Street.

We particularly admired the entrance of BH with its three massive bronze swing doors, which gave into a large, well-lit curved lobby with three 'golden' lifts. At that time they were the fastest lifts in London. To complete the scenic effect of the entrance, above the three bronze doors, there was a sculpture of Shakes-peare's Prospero and Ariel, listening to celestial music standing between Wisdom and Gaiety. However, in 1931, this sculpture by Eric Gill caused much heated discussion because Gill portrayed Ariel as a seven year old boy in full frontal nudity! The critics said that this was disgusting and immoral. We did not agree.

Our office, bearing the number 309, was on the third floor. This was the VIP floor. A couple of doors away were the offices of the Director General, Sir Frederick Ogilvie, and the Chairman of the BBC. We came across the DG by pure chance during our third week in BH. We were coming up from the studio and he was walking to the reference library a few doors further on. I expected to see another tall, dour Reith, but instead I met a courteous gentleman who was ob-viously pleased to meet us. "Oh, you are the Hellenes" he said charmingly. "It's nice to have the descendants of Aristotle and Pericles next to me. You know, I was a classical scholar."

Ogilvie, in fact, was a pure academic and before co-ming to the BBC he had been President of Queen's College, Belfast. For some good reason, I suppose, he had been lured away from academia and asked to take over the tough broadcasting squadron created by Sir John Reith. Ogilvie shook hands with us all, asked about our birth places and then with a charming "hairete" wished us success in our work. I thought it was good to have the DG on our side!

Our office consisted of one large room partitioned into two smaller rooms - quite adequate for six people and three typewriters. Strangely enough, next to us was the Turkish Section. I should explain that to begin with, the Greek Section, for administration purposes, was put into the Near Eastern Department, together with the Arabic, Turkish and Persian Sections. Some wit said that this was as a compliment to Alexander the Great! Anyway, the strange thing was that the typist in the Turkish Section was a young Greek woman called Efrosyne Sideropoulou. In fact Frosso, as we called her, would spend a lot of her spare time in our office in order to talk Greek. She was born in Turkey, in Sinope on the Black Sea, which in the second century BC was part of the Empire of Pontos. Frosso had attended a Turkish school and eventually went to Athens where she took a degree in Greek Literature. After that she came to London and did a post-graduate course in English. At any rate, Frosso could type extremely fast in both Turkish and Greek. Some time later we had Frosso transferred to the Greek Section.

Life at first was novel and exciting because we were learning an entirely new profession and meeting many interesting people from different countries. All three of our announcers were married and lived not far from

BH, so for them getting to work was quite easy. For me, on the other hand, it was a little more difficult. I was married with one child and had decided, some months before the war was declared, that London was no place for my wife and a year old child. I expected the Germans would certainly bomb London. I chose to live in Cambridge, not because I had an affiliation with Cambridge - I myself had been educated at Oxford - but my sister was living at that time in the most beautiful of all English university cities. So I lived in London in rented accommodation and went to Cambridge on my days off.

The BBC was very generous in those early days and to start with they put me up at the Mostyn Hotel, not far from Oxford Street and Portman Square. At the time the BBC was not yet on war footing and it was bedevilled by the problem of finding accommodation for those of its staff who either lived outside London or were too far from BH. In the first two weeks every person, irrespective of job or status, and not living within five miles of BH, was billeted in hotels or furnished rooms. So for a couple of months The Mostyn became home for myself, two other producers, one commissionaire and two messenger boys! Soon, however, when expenses came to be scrutinised by the Controller of Finance, we all left for less luxurious accommodation.

But although we found our work very interesting and often challenging, there was a great deal of nervous tension in our daily lives. After all, the mood of the British people in September 1939 was depressed and negative, reflecting the dispirited attitude and leadership of Neville Chamberlain and his followers.

In London particularly, there was a great deal of apprehension because people had been bombarded with various exaggerated accounts, speculations and warnings. The worst fears were created by the expectation that London could be razed to the ground by high explosive bombs - shades of Guernica - and poison gas bombs. The poison gas posters were very frightening for some people particularly as many of them emphasised that the Germans had used gas in 1916 and the Italians in Abyssinia in 1935. The poster, issued by the Ministry of Home Security, saying "Hitler will send no warning, so always carry your gas mask" was a grim reminder of impending death by gas, emphasised by the gas masks we all carried on our shoulders. So official propaganda intended to advise and protect people also had a negative effect - it created jitters.

Another very depressing event was the evacuation of 1 million schoolchildren, most of them without their parents. This was dubbed operation Pied Piper. One Minister described the evacuation as an exodus bigger than that of Moses. One day I went down to Paddington Station to see some of the evacuees and I was distressed by the sight of many 4 and 5 year olds crying their eyes out because they didn't want to be separated from their parents. This, despite the Government poster which was over the platforms saying, "Mothers, send your child out of London".

At the same time, in some other parts of London, a different kind of evacuation was taking place. This was the evacuation of some two million people who were leaving London completely voluntarily under their own steam, in this case with coaches, cars, vans, taxis, motor bikes and, of course, some very luxurious limousines. It all started in the last days of August and this type of evacuation caused a great deal of antagonism and dissatisfaction. I went up to Hampstead one day to see some of these well-to-do D.I.Y. evacuees. I asked a dear old lady, whose car was loaded with expensive luggage and two fur coats, why she was leaving London? "My dear boy, do you want me to stay here and be blown to bits. Why the hell should I do that? I'm not a cat with nine lives, so I'm off to the green acres of Bucks." Suddenly, it became apparent to me that British society, which had always been an intensely socially divided society, was still so in 1940 and would continue to be despite the war. So those who could afford it decided to leave, locked up their houses and left. Others gave the keys to friends while quite a few houses were simply abandoned to the fate of the war.

Another fear was the blackout. For the first few

days total blackout was a bit of fun, but very soon it became a great personal restriction and a danger to everyone. Total blackout had an amazing psychological effect on your mind. It was like being partially blind. Familiar streets became dark and sinister. You groped your way, you tripped and fell on your face and you could quite easily be run over by a bus or a car. At the time you were told not to use a torch. So the best thing you could do was to stay at home. At any rate there was very little to do because cinemas and theatres were closing and only the pubs were open. So we ventured out in the blackout only when we had to go home. I changed lodgings many times. Sometimes I slept in BBC premises either on a camp bed or in a sleeping bag. Once, by sheer luck, I slept in one of those sumptuous apartments of a block of flats that had been abandoned by their affluent owners. Did I feel guilty? No, I did not!

This was during the so-called phoney war when fear of bombing raids had diminished considerably. An estate agent who knew Bob Dougall - one of the BBC announcers and a good friend of mine - offered Bob a super-luxury flat in Cleveland Row, directly opposite St James' Palace. The whole block of flats was empty, but the agent had the keys to one of the large flats and he offered it to Bob at £15 a month. Beautiful furniture, expensive light fittings, four bedrooms, three large reception rooms, with a fourth in the basement, and three luxurious bathrooms. It also had a superbly fitted kitchen stocked with food for two months. All this for £15 a month! Of course Bob couldn't afford it; so he asked me and Robin Duff to come in with him and share the expenses. We did not hesitate. In a couple of hours we had moved all our belongings - contained in one medium-sized suitcase - and installed ourselves in Cleveland Row like three wealthy lords. Each one of us had, not only his own bedroom, but also his own bathroom. We were in high spirits. "At least, if we get bombed" we said, "we will die among the precincts of St. James' Palace and the news reporters will be looking among the debris for any documents about our distinguished lives for the obituaries."

Our royal residence facing St James' Palace lasted only for two months. After that the entire block was requisitioned by the Ministry of Defence. We three returned to our normal accommodation, which was seldom more than a broom cupboard in one of the BBC buildings. But we had our revenge on the Ministry of Defence. Several months later the famous block of flats took a direct hit and many of the flats were badly damaged in the subsequent flooding. Bob Dougall however was disconsolate. At weekends, while we two were away, he had used our basement super-lounge for some very exclusive parties!

Broadcasting House,
Langham Place
London

CHAPTER 4

VARIOUS PHOBIAS

For the first few days of 1940 we were completely absorbed with problems concerning our broadcasting to Greece. One of the first things we had to decide was what kind of language we were going to use in our bulletins. We had to choose a form of language which would be suitable for talking into the microphone and at the same time easy to hear on short wave. The Greek you write is somewhat different from the Greek you speak. The Greek language the newspapers use is certainly not suitable for broadcasting. We also listened to Athens radio to see how they tackled the problem and we found that their language was pompous and their diction was generally poor, mostly because of reading too fast. So we decided to go in for a simple news format and to develop a clear diction. Keep away from the Rhondiris technique, we said, and let's be natural real people. At first this was difficult, but as we got into the rhythm of broadcasting our voices became rounder and our enunciation improved. And later on, when we were inundated with congratulatory letters, not only from Greece but also from Greek communities of Africa, Australia and North and South America, we knew that we had made the right choice.

Meantime, we had to cope with other problems. The first was how to introduce our programme. We tried various announcements and eventually we chose the simple but arresting Edo Londino Kalispera Sas. One dear lady from a small town in the Peloponnese wrote us a very touching letter. Every night, she wrote, "we gather around the radio to listen to your broadcast. The moment you make your introduction, we reply with Good evening my son, we pray that God will keep you well'".

Then came the microphone neurosis, as we called it. It's strange how intimidating that monstrous bronze object can be to a novice announcer. It sits on its pedestal and just looks at you menacingly. You think it's a carnivorous beast and your hand movements become nervous and spasmodic. Once your hands begin to tremble, then the pages of your script are bound to touch the microphone and the moment a page touches the microphone, a loud explosion is heard. Sometimes it sounds like a pistol shot, sometimes it's like a tyre bursting. It depends where your papers touch the microphone. One night Dino Gregory touched the microphone fifteen times with his papers. This exasperated his colleague, Basil Constantinidis, who was sitting opposite him waiting to read his talk. He pressed the censor key and shouted, "Come on, Dino, for God's sake, are you becoming paralytic?" This caustic remark brought Dino to his senses. He quickly recovered and finished the bulletin in good style. We all applauded.

The announcer had also to learn how to move the pages of his script without losing his place on the next page. We discovered that the only solution to these hazards was to give our nervous announcer a script stand on which to place all his papers. He could then slide the papers noiselessly across the velvet cover of the stand without the pages touching the microphone.

Finally, two other troublesome problems: the studio clock and the speed of reading a script. To the inexperienced Greek announcer, the large studio clock with a red second hand constituted a demonic entity. It was perpetual motion and you could neither stop it nor slow it down and you knew that if you miscalculated the duration of your script, you would overrun and suddenly the clock would read 7.59 and 40 seconds.... the blade of the guillotine would swoop down on you and cut you off the air. You were 'dead' in the studio because the studio itself was dead. The channels switched and a few seconds later another foreign voice would be saying, "Parla Londro Bona Sera" or "Ici Londres, Bonsoir

Chers Amis" while your listeners in Athens would be still waiting to hear the concluding paragraph of your talk. At the same time the voice of the producer in the cubicle would be booming into the studio, "What's the matter, Dino, have you lost your sight? For God's sake can't you see the clock in front of you?". And the announcer would stumble, "Sorry, very sorry boss but I think I'm going blind. I had better go and see a specialist but I'll tell you before I do that, right now I am coming into the studio to smash that bloody clock to pieces, that puppet we have made into a thirteenth Olympian god!" Well, Dino never smashed the clock, but it was a good way to let off steam.

CHAPTER 5

DEMETRIOS CACLAMANOS

I was during early 1940 that I started thinking that the Greek Section, like the German, French and Italian Sections, ought to have its own regular commentator, an eminent personality who would analyse important events as seen by a Greek living in London. Soteriadis, with whom I discussed the matter, suggested Demetrios Caclamanos, the former Greek Diplomatic Envoy to London, and then Honorary Greek Minister. Caclamanos was a distinguished diplomat known for his liberal ideals and his prolific writings on political and literary subjects. So one afternoon, we went to see him in his small flat in Carrington House in the heart of Mayfair.

The flat was crammed with books and political and artistic periodicals were strewn everywhere. Only his desk was tidy, with pride of place given to a small marble bust of Byron, whose poems Caclamanos had often translated into Greek. He could talk about Thucydides and Venizelos with equal ease as he would talk about Gladstone and Byron - and he would pass his comments with a charming, whimsical humour. He was equally at home in the political and literary worlds of the nineteenth century as he was in the world of today. Caclamanos was a prolific writer on ancient and modern Greece and among his works are two translations of Thucydides.

I thought he was a unique personality and a great find for the Greek Section. His only problem was his extremely bad eyesight. He wore very thick glasses but despite these he could only read a letter if he held it more or less against his glasses. So it was obvious straight away that he could not read at the microphone and that one of our announcers would have to read his talks. Caclamanos accepted the compromise and so, after reading a short introduction himself to his first talk, every other talk was read by one of us. Most listeners, however, thought that it was Caclamanos' voice and that the variations in tone were due to atmospheric conditions or to German jamming, which was quite frequent on certain of our transmissions.

The routine was quite simple. Every Monday I would ring Caclamanos and agree with him the subject of his commentary. He would dictate it to one of his two secretaries and then this would be brought over to our office and Mary Moschona would retype it ready to be broadcast. His talks were read usually by Vrassidas

Capernaros or Panos Callinicos. I think that Callinicos read more than half of the five hundred commentaries, which Caclamanos wrote until he died in 1951. All his talks were broadcast in the evening transmission of Saturday and we called them, "From the Watchtower of London". They usually lasted for just over ten minutes. They were extremely popular and no Saturday broadcast would ever go on the air without a Caclamanos commentary. As one listener in Cape Town wrote, "Caclamanos's commentary every Saturday draws us like a magnet. He puts everything in the right perspective. He is quite brilliant. "When I told Caclamanos how popular his talks were, he always smiled with pleasure and added, "I hope that it gives them hope for the future".

When I occasionally went round to his flat to talk about his weekly commentary our conversation would often drift to the Greek Government in Exile, led by Tsouderos, which at this time was based in London. Caclamanos would never accept that the Government in Exile could possibly exercise the power of a genuinely elected government and, in his typically sarcastic way, he called them "the government of parachutists" - which caused much amusement in certain Greek circles in London.

Occasionally he would invite me to have lunch with him at his club - the St.James club - which was his only extravagance. Otherwise he led a very frugal life, seeing most of his English friends in his flat and offering them a Greek coffee and a biscuit. Caclamanos was always badly off because most of his diplomatic pension went to support his two sisters in Greece, and his only other income was from the Greek Section and from occasional articles he wrote for Fleet Street friends. One evidence of his lack of funds was that he always smoked the small wartime Woodbines, which he would produce over coffee from a silver cigarette case that Venizelos had given him after one of their many international conferences. He loved smoking and, every New Year, I used to visit him and take him a box of one hundred Players No.1, a luxury cigarette, long and thick, which was beautifully packed in a splendid coloured box.

Caclamanos shyly accepted his gift with the words, "But Mr.Angeloglou", he was formal and always called me Mr. Angeloglou, "this is too much, it's a cadeau for a Sultan." He paused and then added, laughing innocently, "I shall have to cut the cigarettes in two, because otherwise they will not fit in my special cigarette case."

Responding to listeners. Here Frosso Sideropoulou answers letters from listeners all over the world.

CHAPTER 6

A FLYING CARPET THAT FAILED TO FLY

Our life in the days of the phoney war, which lasted for about seven months, was generally dull, sometimes boring and occasionally full of anxieties, when we were reminded that the air war was bound to come quite soon. But in January 1940 the skies of Britain were only full of pink, fat flying sausages - the barrage balloons - and the news bulletins began to sound repetitive.

Suddenly, there was great excitement at the BBC. King George and Queen Elizabeth accompanied by Queen Mary, the Queen Mother, were coming to visit Broadcasting House to meet the staff of the Foreign Services, which of course included the Greek Section. At that time the large Arabic Section was our immediate neighbour and occupied three large rooms with inter-communicating doors, one of which connected with the Greek Section. The Arabic Section was mostly staffed by Egyptians, most of whom had been studying in London since 1937. We got on well together.

As for me, it was a pleasure to be able to speak a little Cairene Arabic. The most interesting and amusing of the Egyptians was Fuad, their chief translator, who had been studying Engineering at King's College when he was recruited by the BBC in 1938.

The moment Fuad heard of the impending Royal visit, he came over for chat. He told me he had a brilliant idea. He possessed a fabulous Persian carpet, which long ago adorned the bedroom of one of the favourites of the Sultan in the Palace of Yildiz in Istanbul. He would like, he said, to donate the rare carpet to the gracious royal lady, Queen Mary, who was known among her intimate circle never to refuse a precious gift from an admirer!

I congratulated Fuad on his ingenuity and we discussed how to offer the gift to Queen Mary without offending Her Majesty. After considering various ideas, Fuad decided that the best way was to lay the carpet inside the main door of the Arabic Section so that the Queen Mother would have no alternative but to walk over the carpet as she entered the room. In this way Her Majesty would not only see the carpet but also feel with her feet the exquisite texture of the material.

I thought the idea was very imaginative but somewhat risky. "Fuad", I said, "supposing the Queen Mother does not like the carpet, what do you do?"

Fuad uttered a deep sigh. "Mr George", he said,

"impossible. This is a dream carpet. A superb piece of Persian tapestry which was owned by one of the great Sultans of Turkey and used by his favourite concubine."

I did not argue the case, but I felt uneasy. Fuad, however, cheerfully went ahead with his arrangements. He had all the Arabic Section cleaned, tables polished, smart chairs to replace the ordinary BBC chairs and one large pot of flowers was placed in each room.

Fuad himself bought a new suit for the occasion, had a hair cut and sported a beautiful red rose as a buttonhole. He looked splendid. Next to him the rest of the Arabic Section were very ordinary.

At 11 o'clock the next day the whole of B.H. was bubbling with excitement. Fuad, red in the face, rushed into our Section, "They're here, they're here with an army of officers and police, and Queen Mary is with them! We shall soon see whether she likes the carpet or not, Mr George".

It took quite a few minutes for the King and Queen to come our way. Everyone was keyed up, whispering and beckoning to other Sections. Commissionaires were posted along all the corridors and four security officers were opening and closing doors as the Royal party moved along. As they approached the Greek Section I noticed that Mary Moschona was shaking while on the other side of the door the Egyptian women were gig-

A Greek Press Delegation who visited Bush House, London, the headquarters of the BBC European Service, on 6th July 1950, photographed in the studio after watching a Greek transmission.

Left to right: A. Theodossopoulos (“**Embros**” and “**Estia**”, Athens),
N. Lascaris (“**Vradini**” Athens), I. Ioannides (“**Macedonia**” Salo-
nica). Standing: P. G. Sakellariou (sports journalist) A. Mamakis
(“**Ethnos**” Athens), R. Hayles (British Embassy, Athens).

CHAPTER 7

HOT SUMMER 1940 -
THE BATTLE OF BRITAIN

The summer of 1940 was for us one of the most dramatic and eventful years of the war. In the Balkans the political situation was confused with modified pacts and secret treaties, with only Turkey staying neutral. In Africa the Italians were gathering speed and ambition while the British were falling back. The Axis was victorious everywhere and was beginning to look invincible, especially in the Atlantic which, as Churchill said, was the dominating factor throughout the war. "Never for one moment", he added. "should we forget that everything elsewhere depends on the outcome of the Battle of the Atlantic."

During that unusually hot summer of 1940 I was suddenly upgraded. I never knew why but I was given a bedroom with a bath in the Langham Hotel, which the BBC was now using as an overflow from other buildings. My room was small but very comfortable and quite close to the famous winding staircase of the Langham. On my second night in the hotel I was woken up at 5.30 am by a shrill blast on a whistle followed by a sharp gruff command "Everyone down to the ground floor and at the double. We've got a big German raid on." I jumped out of bed, put on trousers and a shirt and in a few seconds I was running down the Langham's beautifully carpeted winding staircase. We were nervously apprehensive as we listened intently to the scream of the engines of the British fighters, who swept low over the hotel on their way to the south coast.

This was the start of the biggest German air offensive against Britain. Hitler and his advisers had decided that, as a first step to the invasion of Britain, the powerful RAF fighters and their bases had to be destroyed. This would be followed by an intensive air bombardment of London and other large cities. Reichsmarschall Herman Goering, the conceited 'enfant gattee' of the Reich, declared on the 11th July "the defence of southern England will last four days precisely; the Royal Air Force four weeks. We can guarantee the invasion of Britain for the Fuhrer within a month!" Despite our uneasiness, I remember that we burst into laughter when Gregory said "that fellow really is bananas" (AFTOS ENE DIO FORES PALAVOS).

The facts were quite different. The Germans had certain advantages over Britain; they had a small superiority in numbers of aircraft and their bases in France

and Belgium were close to their targets on the south
coast of England. They had divided the Luftwaffe into
three air arms each under seasoned commanders like
Kesselring and Stumfft, with Goering as Commander-in-
Chief. They could muster over three thousand aircraft,
of which over a thousand were fighters, like the Mes-
serchmitt 109, which was the only German aircraft
equal to the Spitfire and the Hurricane.

On the British side the skills of the fighter pilots and
their commanders were superior and we had an air
defence system, which was technically the most advanced
at the time. But, most important, the British pilots were
fighting for their families and their homes under attack
by Germany, who was threatening their very way of life.

Reading again some of my notes in my 1940 Diary I
can relive those amazing days from June to September
1940, when our very lives were at stake. One afternoon
in early September, just after our midday transmission,
for some reason almost the entire Greek Section stayed
behind. They all looked very busy, although there was
really nothing for them to do. It was only a tidying-up
job for Maria - as always, after each transmission.

Outside the sky was a beautiful light blue and the
temperature veered towards 30 degrees - made beara-
ble by a gentle breeze. Manolopoulos was nervously
opening and shutting the windows to let in some fresh
air - although the effort made him feel even hotter! Cal-

linicos was resting lazily in our one and only comfortable armchair, while flipping through the Times, while Capernaros was typing with two fingers on an English typewriter.

Soteriadis broke the silence: "Anyone for a walk," he said, "on this glorious English day?" He pointed at me. I smiled and said, "OK I'll come for a short one".

We went out of the section and walked out of Broadcasting House, which was deathly quiet. We made our way to Regent's Park, which was equally quiet - but cooler. Very few people were walking like us, and few were talking. Regent's Park was quite peaceful. The alert had been on since the morning - silence was now welcome. We had had enough noise during the last months with the anti-aircraft guns going off, accompanied by the fast rat-tat-tat of the Spitfires' guns, but loudest of all was the sound of a group of Spitfires that suddenly dived out of a cloud onto an unsuspecting Messerschmit. Then for several minutes we heard the amazing sounds of the aerial dog-fight in the sky above us. Many times we saw one or other of the planes score a hit, and within seconds the other plane lost a wing and then, trailing smoke, screamed down to earth - while the other plane disappeared. The rat-tat-tat of the guns stopped.

At that moment I forgot whose side I was on - a young, healthy, cheerful man was going to his death -

blown out of the skies - German or English. I suppose it made no difference to the dead fighter pilot. Soteriadis guessed my thoughts. "It really makes no difference then", he said. We walked on in silence.

Suddenly we heard a tremendous thundering noise of anti-aircraft fire, followed seconds later by the thump of exploding bombs. The sky to the south-east became a blur of planes - fighters and bombers. A daylight raid over London had been intercepted.

"My goodness," said Soteriadis "the bastards are coming in dozens - this is a bad sign - something is brewing. I hope that God is with us." I said nothing, but prayed to myself as we hastily left Regent's Park, that Soteriadis was right.

Everyone in Broadcasting House was in a state of deep anxiety. This was the most critical period of the war when Britain was more or less isolated. We had now entered a battle that was unique in the history of air warfare. The air battles had begun at the end of May and increased in intensity and ferocity as the summer wore on. The Luftwaffe threw every fighter and fighter-bomber into the battle, using all their bases in France and Norway. They deployed more than 2,000 aircraft. It was a war of attrition. The good thing was that the Germans were suffering far greater losses than the British. The interesting thing was that most military commentators were beginning to think that, if this situation went on, the Luftwaffe would smash itself well before the RAF was weakened. For the Germans a complete change of objectives and tactics had to be made if there was going to be any substantial progress. This meant two things. It was either an invasion of England, which was very doubtful, or the Germans would try to bomb Britain to bits by day and night raids.

On some pages in my diary from July and August, when Britain was fighting for its life, I noted the German losses, and I found that on each occasion the German losses were more than double the British. In ten days between the 8th and 18th August the Germans lost 363 aircraft as opposed to 181 British plus another 30 lost on the ground of British fighter bases. The most extensive attacks took place on August 15th. The RAF made 1,270 sorties and the Germans lost 75 aircraft as opposed to 50 British.

This was when Churchill paid tribute to the RAF in his speech to the House of Commons in the afternoon of August 20th. "The gratitude of every home in our Island, in our Empire, and indeed throughout the world, except in the abodes of the guilty, goes out to the British airmen, who, undaunted by odds, unwearied in their constant challenge and mortal danger, are turning the tide of world war by their prowess and devotion. Never in the field of human conflict was so much owed by so many to so few."

CHAPTER 8

WALKING DOWN OXFORD STREET

I was Tuesday, 12th September 1940. The daylight raids had lessened and the night bombing of London had started in earnest. The clock on All Souls Church next to Broadcasting House had just struck 5 o'clock in the afternoon. I usually took a break at about this time, before going down to the studio to rehearse and put the final touches to the evening Greek transmission, which went on the air at 7.30 pm.

I walked slowly down towards Oxford Circus and stood in the middle of a deserted Oxford Street looking towards Marble Arch. It was an amazing sight. Not a soul to be seen. Nothing moved. It had been a beautiful, very warm day and now the rays of the setting sun were playing on the windows of the buildings and making strange patterns on the melting tar of the road surface. I stood spellbound gazing at this silent London. Was this a ghost town after last night's raid, had the people abandoned the city and fled? No, certainly not. London was simply taking a late afternoon nap, to recover its energies and its courage ready for the onslaught that would be unleashed in a few hours time. As last night and the night before, the German bombers would again groan their way over the Thames and come to drop their deadly cargoes in these very streets and squares of south and west London. I imagined Hitler shouting in his piercing staccato voice, "If the English bombers attack our cities, we will raze theirs to the ground without mercy, so help us God". These words delighted Goering and Kesselring, who were trying to convince Hitler that, failing an invasion, only saturation bombing would bring the English to their knees.

I shook myself out of my reverie and continued my walk towards Marble Arch. There was a lot of damage, mostly in the side streets. Broken glass was everywhere and here and there small mounds of broken window frames, beams and shattered doors. As I passed Selfridges, I saw that only a rear section of the building had been damaged. But the big clock over the main entrance of the store had stopped at 9.50 pm. That was last night of course. My mind went on racing with unbridled thoughts.

What good news had we broadcast to Greece recently? News that would help lift the anxiety and the gnawing fear that we tried to hide? Instead we impotently watched the inexorable advance of the blitzkrieg through north-western Europe during May, the sudden unexpected collapse of France in June and then the di-

57

saster of the British Expeditionary Force at Dunkirk.

Dunkirk, the amazing seven day battle that Churchill had cleverly turned into a victory. Well, yes, you could of course call it a victory-in-defeat when you save some 400,000 British and Allied soldiers, who were gallantly ferried across the Channel by 97 British warships and by hundreds of little ships - most of them just small motor and sailing boats. Yet this undoubted heroic operation cost the British, apart from loss of material and life, several destroyers and more than a hundred fighters, so necessary for the defence of Britain.

My heart sank when I visited some of the wounded rescued from Dunkirk as they came into hospitals, which had been specially emptied. They were the victims of unpreparedness for war - a war that the Allies were fighting with the weapons and tactics of the First World War, against the Germans with up to date armaments and the strategic use of tanks, supported by strong air cover. At this time the Germans seemed unbeatable. And the French? What chance did those poor buggers have with military and political leaders who still thought in terms of the Maginot line?

And, for that matter, how well was I prepared for war? Why was I here in London about to be bombed and burnt with incendiaries? My home was in Egypt - Egypt which would soon be threatened by a strong Italian army under Marshall Graziani. They would advance from

Libya towards the Nile and the oilfields of the Middle East. Greece, my mother country, in the meantime was being threatened by another Italian force, which that madman Mussolini wanted to colonise and use as a stepping stone into Africa. The Middle East and Africa were Mussolini's objectives - no matter what Hitler wanted. The new glorious Roman Empire! Viva Il Duce! And here was I, deeply involved in this war in the midst of London, now being bombed every day and night.

But we Greeks have always admired the English. We were their allies and so must fight with them - win or lose. But we didn't speak of defeat in our broadcasts to Greece because somehow we didn't believe we could lose the war despite the disasters so far. We believed that, in the end, we would win because Britain and its Empire were strong... with perhaps the help of America, when the Americans realised it would be in their interest to come in on our side. Meantime, this bloody war would finish us, if we had leaders of the calibre of the French! But thank God for Churchill. There was no compromise in the man. However, many British aristocrats were appeasers. And the key word before the war started was appeasement. "Peace in their time, not ours."

Yes, thank God for Churchill again. What an amazing man he was. Every time he spoke, whether it was in the House or on the BBC, his words had an electrifying effect on everyone. I remembered the night he broadcast after the fall of France. It was June 4th and I was in a pub having a drink with some colleagues. Churchill spoke with great emotion "The battle of France is over. I expect the Battle of Britain is about to begin. Let us therefore brace ourselves to our duties and so bear ourselves that, if the British Empire and its Commonwealth last for a thousand years, men will still say, 'This was their finest hour'". Faces that were drawn and haggard before Churchill started speaking were now happy and smiling. Some people stood up and cheered or rushed out of the pub as if they wanted to go and fight there and then. That night I went back to Broadcasting House feeling buoyed up, almost happy. I slept better that night. I am sure many Londoners also did.

I was smiling to myself while I was thinking of all this when suddenly I came face to face with an air raid warden. The first human being I had met since leaving B.H. He was in full uniform and wearing his steel helmet. "Where are you off to young man?" he said "you seem to be in a jolly mood!"

"Oh, I am just taking a stroll and looking at the damage before going on the air. I am a BBC reporter and I was thinking of happier days."

"Alright, but don't forget the sun is going down. And mind how you go near the damaged buildings. And also, put on your helmet young man, will you?" I felt embarrassed and I immediately slipped it on. A great man, that warden, I thought, like all the ARP people, and the firemen, the SR men, and ambulance staff. They die in the midst of fires and water, broken glass and falling buildings; unseen and unrecognised. They are all like that.

I turned and made my way back to Broadcasting House. This time I was walking at a brisk pace. As I passed Oxford Circus I saw two more air raid marshalls and then went past the Langham Hotel which had not been damaged yet. It was one of the many buildings occupied by the BBC and occasionally I slept in the hotel's basement in a sleeping bag like many others.

As I entered the lobby of Broadcasting House, which now looked like a fortified dugout with sandbags piled high and an armed soldier on guard, I met a fellow producer.

"Had a nice Cook's tour?" he asked with a smile. "Yes", I replied, "I came to terms with the war." "Well done, my boy", he replied, "hope I do one day. Fat lot of chance I have." I didn't say anything but made my way down the stairs to the basement studio which was two floors below ground. It was almost 7 pm.

One of my announcers greeted me cheerfully and added, "What's it like up there?" "Depressing", I said, "silent like the Libyan desert." "It won't be for long" he replied, "just a couple of hours and we'll all be dancing a quickstep to Hitler's music."

Mary Moschona, who was typing a couple of pages at her usual high speed, said "Have a cup of tea Angie. Tea cures everything, even depression. I have about twenty cups a day myself." Dear Mary. Easy going Greeks, I thought, who adapt to almost anything and who relinquish Brazilian coffee, their national beverage, for tea. Just imagine light tea, tea with powdered milk! An abomination! Mary returned to her typing. I looked at the clock. Time to see the latest British communique. I read it to myself. "Last night there were further enemy raids on south coastal areas and some enemy aircraft penetrated into south west London. Civilian damage was sustained. Ten enemy aircraft were shot down." How many German bombers, I wondered, really got through last night to cause such extensive damage?

CHAPTER 9

A BED IN THE SKY

The first time I saw 'the bed in the sky', as Maria Moschona had christened the damage inflicted on part of the huge Langham Hotel, I was deeply shocked. I was walking back to BH after my week-ly visit to another BBC building, which before the war had been Marshall & Snellgrove but which now housed the Overseas Services of the BBC, when my eyes fell upon an appalling sight at the Langham. I stopped on the warm marble steps of the All Souls Church - fortu-nately hardly damaged - and tried to visualise what had happened last night to the Langham.

A bomb, probably not more than 500 kilos, had struck the fourth floor on the west side of the hotel. It went through two floors and then exploded on the first floor shattering walls, windows and doors but left exposed to view one of the luxurious double bedrooms, almost untouched except for the large double bed. The explosion had carried the bed half out of the shattered wall leaving it anchored to the lush torn carpet by two legs. So half the bed was in the revealed bedroom and the other half was hanging over Portland Place. A large pink eiderdown and a couple of pink blankets waved like flags in the soft evening breeze. The scene looked like a pre-Raphaelite painting. I stood for minutes gazing at the bed in the sky while my imagination ran riot. But the question that was uppermost in my mind was what happened to the two guests? There were six pink pillows, two on the floor and four torn to pieces on a broken armchair.

But again, what happened to the two guests? There was no blood that I could see on the bed and none on the carpet, which was even more strange. Only two pink slippers and next to them a large broken perfume bottle, together with other toiletries. There were some clothes on the sofa and two beautiful armchairs smashed against the wall. But the thought that disturbed me came back. What happened to the two guests? Did they die while they were asleep or did they die while making love?

"Yes", suddenly said a voice from behind me, "Yes, Georges. But do mortals ever have a choice?"

It was Maurice, one of the French announcers, who was walking back to BH for the evening shift. He took my arm and we walked towards the camouflaged entrance door of BH, tonight guarded by soldiers!

"I know what you are thinking Georges", said Maurice. "You Greeks are a very romantic people".

"Thank you Maurice, yes we are. But I will ask the ARP people to remove the bed. We don't need to be reminded that we have no choice even when we are dead".

"Oui, mon cher, it is really much better not to know."

Interviews were often conclucted away from the studio.

CHAPTER 10

B.H. TO WOOD NORTON AND ALL THAT

The night bombing of London had started in earnest on the 7th September and the heavy raids continued for another 65 nights, broken only on 2nd November by bad weather. Bombs had already destroyed or badly damaged a great many buildings in the West End. Some of the raids started at about 8.30 pm and went on until 5 next morning. An entry in my diary on the 12th September reads: "Tonight it took me 20 minutes to cross over from B.H. to the Langham Hotel", about 20 metres away - where I had a sleeping bag in the basement. " It rained shrapnel all night from the new Ack-Ack guns placed in Hyde Park and Regents Park."

The camouflaged B.H., its ground floor masked by 6 square feet of concrete, stood proudly erect despite the destruction all round. However, on the night of the 18th September, when two large bombs scarred the two streets immediately behind B.H., the Government decided that it was time to protect Britain's precious broadcasting service by evacuating it some 100 miles north west of London to Wood Norton, near Evesham. Wood Norton had been bought by the BBC in April 1939 against the eventuality of war.

At 7.30 am on 19th September about a dozen double-decker red buses - some of them with open tops - lined both sides of Portland Place. The buses quickly filled with young men and women speaking foreign languages and carrying the essentials of their offices - their foreign typewriters plus one piece of personal luggage. We, the members of the Greek Section, together with the Portuguese, chose the open top of a London Transport bus, while the Arabs and the Persians filed into the lower deck. Once we got going our enthusiastic typist, Mary Moschona, with a portable Greek typewriter on her lap, started typing material for our mid-day bulletin. It was a bright sunny September morning and, as we went through the deserted streets of north London, we all thought that we were very lucky. In a few hours we would be in the midst of the green fields of Evesham and not in some dingy, claustrophobic basement in London.

Wood Norton was a large country house, surrounded by 5 acres of grassland. The house had been rebuilt at great expense in the 1890's by the exiled Duc d' Orleans and the fleur-de-lis motif was in profusion in all the main rooms and bathrooms. But, unfortunately, accommodation was limited as others were already there, and our sleeping quarters were in one of the many corrugated iron huts which had been put up by the Royal Engineers in the vast grounds of Wood Norton. Our hut was sandwiched between two others, one housing the Portuguese Section and the other the Arabic Section. I was born in Cairo and spoke quite good Arabic, so I got on quite well with the Arabs, most of whom were Egyptians. The only snag was that many of them spent half the night playing poker on a wooden table placed outside our door. The clanging of half crowns and shillings on the wooden table, plus the loud, excited bidding made sleep very difficult; so quite often some of us joined in the lively, high spirited gambling. This was a welcome relaxation after the tensions and dangers of London.

A few days after our arrival in Evesham two members of the Greek Section - who we called the Cypriot contingent - and who had missed the first part of the evacuation, arrived to join us. This group consisted of Michael Cacoyannis and Beba Clerides.

I do not remember what Beba did for lodgings but I always remember the shock that Michael suffered when he realised that he had to sleep on an iron camp bed in an army hut. He found the accommodation completely primitive and thought that his health would suffer! So after sleeping one night in 'this ghastly metal bed', he borrowed a bicycle and cycled 12 miles to come and see me in my home. At the time I was living with my wife and two-year-old son in the charming Cotswold village of Chipping Campden where we rented a small cottage with the romantic name of Barley Mow. Michael arrived as it was getting dark and when I opened the door he nearly collapsed on our doorstep. He had cycled the 12 miles, mostly uphill, and was physically shattered. He asked if he could spend the night "anywhere" he said, even on the bare flagstones rather than go back to the awful conditions of Wood Norton. My wife immediately said that we had a spare bed and Michael could spend the night with us. Anyhow, I think Michael was so exhausted that he would have slept anywhere - even in an armchair.

The next day Michael went back to Evesham and managed to find himself a room in one of the local hotels, which also provided him with baths and meals. So Cacoyannis set new standards in living conditions for the BBC evacuees of Evesham!

Talking about evacuees in this period of 1940 reminds me how we - that is my wife and I - were at first greeted at Chipping Campden. At that time some of the papers carried exaggerated stories about German spies in civilian clothes being dropped by parachute to assist Hitler's invasion of the British Isles. Some of these stories had worried the inhabitants of this somewhat isolated and hilly area of the Cotswolds and when two foreign strangers - that is my wife and I - arrived at

Chipping Campden we were looked upon with a great deal of suspicion. That is before we had informed the village that I was a BBC man. I remember one evening we went into one of the local pubs for a quick drink. The moment we entered there was a complete hush and everybody stood looking suspiciously at the two of us. My wife got very worried and wanted to go home. We left in a few minutes, and the moment we shut the door the whole pub came to life again.

I heard one voice saying "She must be German, a blonde, and he a dark man probably an Italian!" We were very upset and my wife started thinking that we should leave Chipping Campden. The next day I went to see the local vicar. He was a charming friendly old boy with an equally charming wife and he said that he would immediately talk to the village and explain who we were. In fact, the vicar went out that night and talked to members of the parish council. Two days later my wife and I were invited to have a drink at the same pub. Everyone was very jolly and friendly and many said that they were pleased to have BBC evacuees in Chipping Campden. I realised that the BBC was even more powerful in the Cotswolds than it was in London.

Our work, which at first was hampered by a lack of teleprinter machines and other technical problems, soon became quite pleasant. It was an open-air life - our office overlooked a cornfield. Although living conditions were a bit primitive, food was fresh and good and the nationalities mixed extremely well. In fact, Wood Norton showed that people speaking different languages and coming from completely different social and religious backgrounds, can get on together and work harmoniously. The situation leads to lasting friendships and occasionally torrid love affairs. For the first time, we Greeks met and mixed with English, French, Germans, Spaniards, Portuguese, Poles, Czechs, Arabs and Turks to mention only a few. It was the start, so to speak, of a new League of Nations, which later developed into the important and talented European Service when we moved into Bush House in March 1941. And London, with its deadly air raids, seemed so far away that sometimes we all felt we were broadcasting from another country.

But one or two people were highly disturbed with our announcements of "This is London Calling". In fact, one member of the Greek Section, Nionio Damiris refused to broadcast and threatened to resign. He said it was dishonest to pretend that we were in London. Eventually our manager and I succeeded in persuading him that it was simply for security reasons we were not disclosing our whereabouts. Little did our righteous Greek announcer know that already "Gairmany Calling", that is Lord Haw Haw, was ridiculing us by saying that the B.B.C. was now talking from the wilds of the

Vale of Evesham. A few days later, while we were preparing our mid-day bulletin in our "conservatory" office, the alert was sounded and three German fighter bombers circled very low over Wood Norton preparing to do a bomb run. One of the pilots looked as if he was giving us the Nazi salute! We, in the meantime, had all run into the cornfield preparing to die for the sake of our cause! Suddenly, as if by a miracle, half a dozen Spitfires appeared and in a few seconds the Germans did an about-turn, jettisoned their bombs on three greenhouses about half a mile away and disappeared pursued by the Spitfires.

We all emerged, very shaken, from the ditches of the cornfield but soon we were discussing with others whether it was better to be bombed or to be straffed. First thing next morning my recalcitrant Greek announcer came to see me and apologised for all the fuss he had made about "This is London Calling" from Evesham. We became very good friends after that.

The Wood Norton "lie", was caricatured in a clever ditty, which also made fun of the changing character of the BBC at war:

> " Once any taint of misdemeanour
> Upset the Corporation's tenour;
> But times have changed almost completely;
> 'Tis now no sin to sin discreetly

And final sign of moral falling -
Evesham may say it's "London Calling".

As a result of the abortive German raid, the defences of Wood Norton were immediately strengthened and access to most areas was restricted. We suffered no further air raids but we eye-witnessed, from a distance of about twenty-five miles, the devastating bombing of Coventry on the 14th and 15th November 1940. I shall never forget sitting up all night seeing Coventry being blasted from the air. On the first night the Germans used 500 long- range bombers and they came in waves for ten solid hours to rain high explosives and incendiaries on Coventry. They ravaged the City centre, gutted the Cathedral, damaged aircraft factories and killed and injured hundreds of people. At certain times the anti-aircraft guns stopped firing either because of lack of ammunition or because their barrels were too hot to continue. And the next night the bombers came back again to finish off what they had started.

Two days later, Soteriadis and I went into Coventry to report on the appalling damage, we were so deeply shocked that neither of us could speak. We just stared at the mangled debris and at the faces of the survivors etched with pain and exhaustion. And yet no-one seemed to complain and there were no tears. Throughout the day gallant firemen, policemen and soldiers were desperately busy trying to restore some sort of order in the chaos that was facing them, so that Coventry could survive. And bravely it did survive.

In the meantime came the massive Italian attack on Greece. On the 28th October Mussolini's crack divisions and mechanised brigades invaded Greece from Albania. People thought that little Greece had no chance against such a powerful and well- equipped army. It was the giant versus the pygmy. Yet in a few days, the small well- disciplined Greek army repulsed the Italian attack, and ten days later the Italian divisions were falling back into Albania in disgrace.

For us this was stupendous and exhilarating news, but the war with Italy caused a great logistical problem for us. Wood Norton was suddenly too isolated and too far from London and we needed closer liaison and advice from both the British and the Greek official sources. So on the 15th November, the Ministry of Information, with our connivance, decided to move the Greek Section back to London well before the other language groups came to return. Where to? Well, to B.H. again. And here began another unforgettable chapter in the life of the Greek Section.

CHAPTER 11

FROM WOOD NORTON TO B.H. TO MAIDA VALE AND FINALLY TO BUSH HOUSE

The Greek Section left the green acres of Wood Norton on Tuesday, 19th November 1940, in advance of other European Sections and we came back to the camouflaged building of B.H., which by now had been renamed Battleship Broadcasting House. B.H. was painted deep grey and buttressed on the lower levels, and did look very much like a battleship ready to sail down Regent Street. In fact, "the battleship" had suffered its first direct hit on the night of October 15th, when a 500 lb delayed action bomb went through the wall on the seventh floor and came to rest at the door of the music library on the fifth floor. It exploded a few minutes later just as the announcer was reading the 9 o'clock news in a basement studio, with plaster from the ceiling cascading down on his script. The destruction was quite extensive and seven members of staff were killed. The damage, however, was repaired quickly but after that, every night an armoured car waited outside B.H. ready to take the news announcer to the BBC Studios in Maida Vale in case of another direct hit. The Greek Section was, of course, in Evesham at the time.

When we arrived back at B.H. we were given an office on the third floor - it was Room 309, which is today a small private dining room. We also had a second office in the basement, which we used during air raids. We had resettled quite well to the arduous existence in an overcrowded B.H., often sleeping in converted offices and spare rooms of adjacent buildings.

At night the large Concert Hall was converted into a makeshift dormitory with small mattresses and dozens of pillows and blankets. But the Puritan spirit of Sir John Reith dictated that men and women should be segregated. To do this, the House Manager created partitions with blankets thrown across strong nylon ropes, thus creating flimsy partitions between men and women. Men on the left and women on the right. This separation of the sexes caused a lot of amusement and a couple of practical jokers added to the fun on certain occasions, by cutting the ropes, in this way collapsing the walls of Jericho on the sleeping females!

For a time Broadcasting House life was routine and certainly dull and difficult. Suddenly the big blow fell. It was Sunday night, 8th December 1940. London was having one of its heavy night raids. At about 10.30 pm, while I was waiting with many others in the foyer of B.H. for a lull in the raid, a one ton land mine gently floated down under a large green parachute over Portland Place. Someone shouted that a German pilot had bailed out and a policeman and two A.R.P. wardens rushed out to arrest the German pilot. A few seconds later, the land mine silently landed in Portland Place about 2 metres from the wall of the building. There was a deafening explosion. It destroyed the concrete blocks which strengthened the sides of the building and also made a huge hole in the street, shattering the basement walls. Masonry crashed down from the second and third floors, fires started and, worst of all, water pipes burst, flooding large areas on the ground and underground floors. The entrance hall soon began to look like a small lake.

Still dazed by the explosion, I managed to scramble down to our room in the basement. To my horror, I found that our office was already knee-deep in water. All the files were soaked and things were floating around the room. I just managed to rescue my 1940 BBC diary, which is my one memento of that horrendous night.

Soon after, the decision was taken to evacuate B.H. As bad luck would have it, most of the foreign language staff were ordered to move to the former Ice Rink, which had been converted to emergency studios, named

Maida Vale Studios. The painful move was done in the early morning after the raids had finished.

Maida Vale Studios were on one level - with a kind of basement that housed the boiler room. It was a ramshackle, inadequate, noisy, overcrowded building, which offered no protection at all from the bombs. The roof, most of which was made of glass, and the walls of the building were so thin that we could often hear people talking in the street. Secretaries would stop typing the news bulletins in order to hear whether the next stick of bombs would be a hit or a miss! One day, one of the English secretaries became so angry that she put on her coat and steel helmet and walked out of the building shouting, "So long suckers. Our bosses herd us together like cattle. If Hitler is going to get me I'd rather be out in the open air than have all this muck falling on top of me".

We were working in tiny offices, in very cramped conditions, with obsolete equipment and under the constant threat of being killed or maimed. This made life for all staff anything but cheerful or conducive to good work. And the war news during that period was not particularly jubilant either. Although we had won the Battle of Britain at a great cost, the fall of France, Dunkirk, and the continuing threat of an invasion and the tremendous losses of allied merchant shipping to U-boats brought home to us the power of Nazi Germany.

Furtive thoughts of the possibility of defeat were pushed away into the subconscious.

The Greek Section on the other hand was brighter than most; we were at least broadcasting news of the amazing victories of the small Greek army against the Italian divisions which had now been forced back some 40 kilometres into Albania. This gave us a great filip. But to be truthful, these amazing Greek victories were hundreds of miles away and therefore only provided a temporary tonic to our weary bodies and brains.

Altogether, our stay in Maida Vale was sheer purgatory. Although bombs did not score a direct hit on Maida Vale while we were there, going to and from Delaware Road each night was a dispiriting experience, especially if we passed recent destruction or came across people injured by shrapnel from our anti aircraft guns. For this reason, many of us started using the Underground. But here again, the atmosphere was melancholy.

As you made your way down to the station platforms - now reduced to about two feet in width - you came upon scores of women, children and old men, lying close to each other on makeshift mattresses, half dressed covered by a blanket or rug. They looked desperately uncomfortable and yet they were all grateful to be safe 30 metres below ground.

Before the start of the Blitz, Underground stations

in central London were locked at about 11 pm. A few days after the Blitz started, because of a great public outcry, supported by the Press, the Government gave orders that all tube stations must leave their gates open and only close them if there was danger of overcrowding. This was the first demonstration of people power in Britain! As a result, some 80 underground stations were eventually fitted with bunks and facilities. The "bombed out" at the end of the Blitz totalled one million people, at a time when London's population was nine million.

By a miracle, we survived in Maida Vale until February 1941 when at last we made our third and final move to Bush House in Kingsway - at the top of the Strand. We were very lucky because two weeks after we left Maida Vale the building received a direct hit with one person killed and several wounded!

Everyone greeted our move to Bush House with tremendous relief. Bush House was not only a large and imposing building with several wings, but it was also a safer place in comparison to the glass roofed Maida Vale Studios. But the real importance of Bush House was that it became the vital turning point in the history of the Foreign Services of the BBC. It completed the creation of a British broadcasting organisation, which forcefully delivered the allied message to occupied Europe and eventually helped to overwhelm the powerful

Part of the editorial room of the Greek Section, where a bulletin is being prepared for transmission.
Left to right: Antony Mitsidis, George Angeloglou, Georgina Wood and Yvonne Lane.

and evil propaganda machine of the Third Reich.

As the Greek Section grew in size and importance and its broadcasts were increased to six a day we were joined by a number of very able men and women among whom I should mention; Panos Callinicos, Vrassidas Capernaros, Dionyssis Damiris, Stelios Democratis, Mimis Manolopoulos, George Megarefs, Petros Marsellos, Aristotelis Sismanidis, Costas Mylonas, Hector Tembros, Panos Bakirtzis and Kakos Kyriakidis. Georgina Wood joined Frosso Sideropoulou, along with other young women who acted as Greek secretaries.

CHAPTER 12

YEIA SOU - WE ARE THE GREEKS
OF THE TWENTIETH CENTURY

When, on the 28th October 1940, Mussolini launched his major attack on Greece through southern Albania, people in Britain and in fact in the rest of the free world shook their heads and thought that Greece was completely doomed. However, in just two and a half weeks the Greek army, with only about half the strength and equipment of the Italians, launched a powerful counter attack. The Italians neither expected nor thought it was possible in view of Greece's military weaknesses. In fact, the ferocious and highly efficient Greek counter attack came like a whiplash, which cut the Italian armies in half and sent them retreating into Albanian territory to avoid being surrounded. This was the beginning of the Italian retreat, which later surrendered to the Greeks several key towns, amongst them Korytsa, Pogradecz, Argyrokastro, Tepelen, Klissoura and Chimara. The Italian withdrawal gave the Greek army considerable quantities of military equipment as well as prisoners, and made Italian communications extremely hazardous.

Although Greece was always pro-British, and traditionally allied to Britain, at the start of the war very few people in Britain knew very much about Greece or had ever been there. In fact in London and Cardiff Greek grocers had to put up huge posters in their windows saying, ' This is a GREEK shop - not ITALIAN' to avoid having their windows broken by angry anti-Italian demonstrators. Later, when the Greeks threw back the Italian advance the Greeks suddenly became the heroes of the day and the British people tried to show their support and pride in every possible way.

In pubs people learnt to say "Geia sou" and "Zeto", taxis hooted the V-sign and Greek flags appeared on buildings and in the streets. Shop windows displayed enlargements of some witty and anti-Italian cartoons by famous cartoonists like Low, Vicky, Strube and Illingworth. One particular popular cartoon from the Daily Mail depicted an Italian army unit marching backwards towards Albania with Mussolini at its head, also riding backwards, not on a white charger but on a black mule.

In Piccadilly, the Monsignor news theatre was showing the latest newsreels, but you had to queue to get into the theatre. It was a joy to see these films. One showed the triumphant entry of the Greek army into

83

Korytsa; another showed the fierce fighting in the nar-
rows of Klissoura and a third newsreel followed Epirote
women climbing up a mountainside carrying guns and
food to soldiers in the front lines. This sequence was
particularly moving, especially when one of the women
was wounded by Italian gunfire and the other women
rushed to her help. The audience burst into applause,
while shouting "bravo, well done, zeto".

One evening a group of us from the Greek Section
went into a popular pub near Broadcasting House. We
were speaking Greek and we obviously attracted people's attention. A few minutes later the publican came
from behind the bar and smilingly said "I know you are
Greeks because five years ago I was in the Merchant
Navy and I learnt a bit of Greek in Cardiff. I must say
that we are all very proud of you Greeks. You're champion fighters, so let me offer you a drink to celebrate
the amazing thrashing you are giving to old Musso!"

At that point other customers came over and joined
us and in a few minutes everyone in the pub was holding
a glass to drink a toast to the Greek Army and the Greek
people. The gruff voice of the publican shouted "Cheers
lads, three cheers for the Greek soldiers in Albania who
are showing the Italians how to fight". And the entire
pub exploded in Zetos and Geia sou and applause.

Meanwhile, in Albania, the Italian army had continued to retreat to what they called 'more advanta-

geous positions'. General Sodu, Commander in Chief in Albania, was relieved of his command and was replaced by Ugo Cavallero. But in January and February 1941 came the most severe winter for many years in Albania with temperatures dropping down to minus 15C. The Italians suffered more than the Greeks as most of the Italian units came from southern parts of Italy and had trained in a warmer climate. At the time of broadcasting, we certainly had no accurate figures for frostbite and pneumonia, but it now seems reasonable to say that the extreme temperatures caused 12,000 casualties for the Italians and about 7,000 for the Greeks.

In London, and in all other big cities, the British and Greek Red Cross combined with other war relief organisations to send food, and especially warm clothing, to the Greek soldiers in Albania. In my diary, I have a note saying that in one week in January 1941 six plane-loads of supplies were sent from London alone. One of the planes was carrying a consignment of one million M&B anti-biotic tablets. M and B are the initials of the pharmaceutical firm of May & Baker, which produced this forerunner of penicillin, the wonder drug which followed soon after.

As a means of collecting funds, the Greek War Relief Fund and the Greek Red Cross combined to give a magnificent show of song, music and extracts from current plays at the London Palladium on January 18th 1941. It was called Midnight Matinee It started at midnight and ended at 4 a.m. Over one hundred well-known actors, singers, conductors and musicians came to the Palladium to give a performance after they had finished their own shows. The huge theatre was packed to the ceiling. Royalty was there, among them Princess Marina and, of course, politicians, diplomats and representatives of the Allied Forces and the London Greek community. In fact, everyone who mattered was there. The atmosphere was one of elation and high spirits. The participants, especially Laurence Olivier, Noel Coward and Douglas Fairbanks - who introduced the concert - gave moving tributes to the Greek soldiers who, as Fairbanks said, were two feet deep in snow but still chasing the Italian Blackshirts up and down the hills of Albania.

But the highlight of the show was the star singer, Florence Desmond, who sang "What a surprise for the Duce, he can't put it over the Greeks". This was a satirical ditty which made a laughing stock of Mussolini and his pompous prattle that he would conquer Greece in one week - and enter Athens on a white charger. The audience absolutely loved it and after the first encore, everyone joined in the singing. At the end of each refrain, there was a delirious ovation with people standing, applauding, throwing flowers on the stage and shouting "More, more, Flo, more!" After the fifth or sixth encore - I can't remember which - an emotionally drained but radiant Florence came to the edge of the flower-strewn stage and spoke to the audience. "Thank you, thank you, everyone, very much. You are all having a wonderful time I know and I am gradually losing my voice! I think that after this, I should really fly to Athens and sing this song to those brave Greek boys at the front. They deserve your applause; not me."

To prevent any further encores, the theatre orchestra rose to its feet and struck up the National Anthem of Greece followed by the British one! As evidence, I still have the lacquer disc, which the BBC recorded during that unforgettable night in 1941. This was indeed a very moving tribute to Greece and its people. I suppose very few now remember a speech given by Ernest Bevin in 1946 to the United Nations Security Council. Bevin rose and in his raucous voice said, " We want to remind the world that from 1940 to 1941, with the exception of the British Empire, Greece was our only fighting ally who opposed the enemy and defeated Italy. We must not allow ourselves to forget it to-day". I personally wonder whether to-day any of the United Nations even remember what Greece did in the last war.

But although such cheerful and heartening events like the Midnight Matinee helped to bolster up the morale of the Greek Section, all members were aware that we were sitting on top of a volcano. One very disturbing thing was the tremendous shortage of food in Greece and especially in Athens. We received various reports that people, and especially children, were dying in the streets during the severe winter of 1941. Quite a lot of pathetic photographs were smuggled out of Greece and were soon published widely in Britain, America and Egypt. I well remember one of the most gruesome photographs was a shot of some thirty people huddled together over the large extractors of the underground station at Omonia Square. Most of them were old men and young children and they looked as if they were shivering out the end of their lives. Maria Moschona was so shocked by this picture that for three days she could not even drink tea without milk! Amazingly, a few days later came a news flash, which cheered everyone. The item was entitled "Food for Greece".

"Agreement has been reached between Britain, U.S.A. and Turkey to supply limited quantities of food to Greece. British blockade policy was not affected as produce came from Turkey. The Turkish ship 'Adana' was due to sail from Istanbul to Piraeus on September 15th with the first shipment of 50,000 tonnes of wheat, pulses and eggs. The food was distributed in Greece by the Vanderbilt Committee, the Turkish Red Cross and the International Red Cross."

We broadcast this in all our bulletins on September 10th and we gave further details of the shipments all next day. The famine in Greece, and especially in Athens, had been covered extensively in many of our bulletins and commentaries and we always gave as many details as were available in London and Cairo. Meanwhile photographs had reached London and had been published in newspapers causing a great upsurge of sympathy from ordinary people. Then, on page 258 of my diary of 1941, I see a note that I wrote on September 15th:

> "***Food for Greece***. *Simopoulos, the Greek Ambassador, rings this morning to say that according to the Foreign Office, our broadcasts of the 10th and 11th September, regarding the food supplies to Greece, had been badly received by the German Embassy in Ankara. The Germans object to the publicity we have given to the fact that the British and Greek government in exile are also involved in these shipments. The Germans threaten to stop further shipments unless the Greek broadcasts of the BBC go slow on the whole matter. Simopoulos suggests that we can now go slow as we have already given sufficient publicity and the whole of Greece will know the facts. So we decide to lay off for a few days!*"

The shipments of food, though somewhat slowed down, went on and continued to make things easier for the people of Greece.

CHAPTER 13

ENCOUNTER WITH GENERAL DE GAULLE

T was at the time of the great victories of the Greeks against Mussolini's invasion army. By the second week of November 1940, the Greeks had pushed back the crack Italian divisions into Albania and had captured several key communication centres and performed what people thought was a military miracle. The entire free world was singing the praises of Greece and its soldiers.

One evening, I was rushing down to the basement studio for our evening transmission. I was late and had forgotten to check the number of the studio, which quite often changed at short notice. Normally, our studio was number 14 so I went towards that particular studio. I remember I was wearing a dark grey suit and a white shirt, and therefore I looked reasonably senior grade. I pushed open the studio door and to my great astonishment there, in front of me, stood the monolithic figure of General de Gaulle, in the sparse Free French uniform, adorned only with the Cross of Lorraine.

De Gaulle looked sombre and irritated. He was expecting the Czechoslovakian ambassador to do a talk and the ambassador was late. "Monsieur l' Ambassadeur", he snapped at me, "vous etes en retard." I went pale. I gulped. "General de Gaulle, je m'excuse. Je suis Grecque." De Gaulle's face lit up when I started to explain who I was. He grabbed my hand and shook it vigorously. "Ah, you wonderful Greeks, tell your compatriots when you go on the air that they are superb, gallant fighters. We, the Free French, salute them. We are certain that soon the Duce and his armies will be swimming for their lives in the Albanian Sea!"

He laughed with delight and then accompanied me to the studio door which was held open by that talented politician, Maurice Schumann, who also offered his congratulations. We shook hands again. Then I ran down the corridor where I saw two of my announcers standing outside studio 12 and waving me on. "You are late", they said. I smiled. At that moment it didn't really matter if I was late. I was feeling as tall as de Gaulle!

CHAPTER 14

LOVE UNDER THE BILLIARD TABLE

IN March 1941, a very kind friend and colleague, gave me the use of his flat for a month while he was away in Scotland recording a programme. It was a comfortable one-room bachelor flat in Kensington Close, just off the High Street.

My move to Kensington coincided with resumption of the blitz after a lull of some weeks. As luck would have it, Goering decided to give the centre of London a bit of his nightly medicine. Most of the residents of Kensington Close, mostly women working for the ministries, decided that they would sleep in the long corridors rather than in their rooms to avoid being showered with broken glass and to have quieter nights. So I, too, on the advice of my next door neighbour, moved my mattress into the large 'dormitory'. My neighbour was a slim, tall young woman in her late twenties, called Zoe. She had a delicate oval face, a sensuous mouth, and the most attractive liquid blue eyes I'd ever seen. With her ready smile and a happy laugh, I was instantly attracted to her. We talked a lot and always had a small drink before bedding down in the corridor 'dormitory'.

Two nights later, when I went up to the corridor, Zoe was not there. A note on my door said that she had discovered a better and quieter place to sleep. It was the billiard room, sandwiched between the restaurant and the snack bar. A large room, without windows but with good air conditioning. I found Zoe on a mattress below one of the two large billiard tables! She looked cheerful and cosy. "It's great here", she said, "and certainly no glass windows. The management provides the mattresses and some blankets and you bring your pillows!" She laughed. It was already late. The raid had been on for some time and ack ack explosions reverberated round the walls of the billiard room. It was going to be a bad night and sleep was difficult. At about 2 a.m. I got up, went to the kitchen of the snack bar to make some tea. I brought Zoe a large mug and gave her two aspirins. After that she went to sleep quite peacefully.

The next day we heard the bad news. The West End had got it badly, Marble Arch, Oxford Street, Leicester Square. One of the worst was the destruction of the Cafe de Paris next to the Rialto Cinema in Coventry Street and two floors underground. And yet two bombs went through four ceilings and landed on the dance floor of the Cafe de Paris in the basement. The Cafe de Paris was a popular night-club frequented by service men on leave and their girlfriends. That night the explosion of one bomb - the other didn't explode - in an underground enclosed space killed thirty three people on the dance floor and badly injured another sixty. Five of the men who died while dancing were Spitfire pilots. One of the girls who died was a friend of Zoe.

When we met next evening, Zoe was pale and her eyes were swollen. She was very subdued and conversation was difficult. I gave her a drink and at about 10 o'clock we went to the billiard room and our mattresses. The raid was already at its peak and the ack ack guns, not far away, were in continuous action. She grasped my arm and whispered in my ear. Is it bad like last night? I said yes and softly kissed her cheek. She snuggled closer. She was weeping silently. Our bodies were now touching flesh to flesh. Suddenly there was a gigantic explosion. The building shook violently, some plaster fell on to the billiard tables and nearby windows were smashed to pieces. Zoe put both arms around me and her face on my cheek. She was trembling. A number of people got up and got out of the room. A few minutes later a warden walked in. "It's alright" he said, "it was a land mine, but it fell next door on the Hospital in Marloes Road. Your building is OK. Just stay where you are, but don't try to go upstairs. It's all a great mess".

I went to the bar and got a glass of water and some more aspirins. Zoe was now quiet. We were the only people in the billiard room as the others had not returned. Suddenly Zoe came very close to me. "Please make love to me, please". She said it very softly, very tenderly; it was almost an entreaty from the heart. She tried to cover my mouth with her lips as if to prevent a negative reply. There was no negative reply. Zoe gave a cry. A soft, sweet, long cry, mingled with tender words of love, some almost incoherent. Then a long kiss that searched to find tenderness and ecstasy. It lasted for some minutes and then it eventually subsided. She rested her face against mine, her arms holding me tightly.

When the all clear went at about 5 in the morning, we were still entwined, but dead to the world. Apparently no-one had come into the billiard room, not even the warden! We spent a wonderful week of love and intimacy, despite the awfully depressing news of the war. When the raids became lighter, we moved up into the long corridors and then into Zoe's flat.

Just before my colleague came back from Scotland, Zoe went up to Liverpool to see her mother who had gone down with very bad bronchitis. A few days later, Liverpool had a bad night raid. It was the 27th March. Zoe was caught in the streets when the anti-aircraft guns were blazing at the German bombers. It was literally raining shrapnel that night and Zoe ran into a metal storm without a helmet. She was taken to hospital, but she died a few hours later.

I learnt of her death next morning. The great shock numbed my brain and my body. My eyes were dry but my heart wept all day. When night came, I went out and began walking the streets of Kensington. I walked for hours looking at the skies. But on that night, the skies of London were empty and quiet. London had no raid at all!

CHAPTER 15

THE PRIMAVERA OFFENSIVE - 1941

After the disasters he had suffered in Albania during the first four months of the war against Greece, Mussolini now decided that he must prove to Hitler that he was a great tactician and his forces were invincible. Foolishly he forgot that his troops had gone through a bitter winter with temperatures of minus 15C to 20C and that for one month, most casualties on the front were from severe frostbite.

The Greek Section became nervous because Mussolini had now amassed a force of more than 7 divisions, 300 large guns plus aircraft. The only difficulty for Mussolini was that most of his army was newly trained and their training had been done in the hills of Umbria and Tuscany, and not in Albania.

It was Gregory who spread the nervousness by saying that the odds now looked like 6 to 1 against the Greeks and the weather was getting milder. On the 9th March Mussolini opened the spring offensive himself by firing the first shot on the ten kilometre front. He watched the action through a huge black telescope. He was looking at 7 crack divisions, some 300 heavy guns and about 500 aircraft, most of which could not take off because of the awful weather conditions.

For three hours the Italians attacked with heavy artillery and then followed it with infantry attacks which broke against the Greek lines and the well fortified hills, some of which became famous in the next two or three days. Among these hills was Hill 731, which was attacked twelve times. Each attack was repulsed and brought to a bloody standstill. On one night, the 11th and 12th of March, two battalions of Black Shirts which had infiltrated a defile in an attempt to outflank Hill 731 - the symbol of Greek resistance - were completely wiped out by Greek artillery. Prisoners were now being taken easily. No-one counted the dead.

And so the unfortunate Italian spring offensive progressed. On the 12th March the Italian Commanders changed their tactics. The Bari division was brought up and added considerable losses to the three divisions already involved. The battles had no effect on the impregnable positions of the Greeks who always had the great advantage of being positioned on the high hills looking down on the Italians.

For the next few days the Italian infantry attacks continued interrupted only by massive bombardments and air attacks. Hill 731, very high and proud, rose out of the smoke like an invincible pyramid in this wild landscape ruled over by destruction and death. On the seventh day, the Italian destruction continued. Mussolini, seeing the worsening situation and the increasing number of Italian losses, realised that his forces were now facing complete defeat. Mussolini - in typical fashion - lost his temper and started cursing his commanders, including of course the unfortunate Caballero.

The gradual destruction of the Italian crack regiments in the course of days was completely unexpected. We just couldn't believe it. At times we almost felt sorry for the Italians because it was obvious that they were now very weary, completely discouraged and totally demoralised. On March 15th, the seventh day of the offensive, Mussolini witnessing the defeat of his forces realised he was losing. He became quite alarmed and burst into violent abuse of his commanders. A few hours later, Mussolini decided to leave the front and went to the hospital in Valona, where his daughter was lying injured from a torpedo attack.

This was really the end of Mussolini as a Commander-in-Chief. At any rate, Mussolini was now overtaken by more significant events. In about three weeks, on 6th April 1941, four German army corps crossed the Greek borders with Bulgaria and Yugoslavia. This was one of the worst moments in our broadcasting to Greece. The Italian forces were now written off; from being a strong attacking army that was expected to support Hitler in his conquest of Europe, they had now become a crushed and leaderless army, whose only hope to escape destruction was to withdraw further into the wilds of Albania!

CHAPTER 16

DIARY ENTRIES   APRIL 1941

April 1941 was one of the most dramatic and tragic months in the history of modern Greece. It began with the final German preparations for the invasion of Greece and Yugoslavia. On Sunday 6th April, German armoured forces entered Greece through Bulgaria, while Belgrade was being heavily bombed. Yugoslav resistance collapsed quite quickly. The Greeks, better equipped and far more experienced in war, fought gallantly in the Struma valley and fought to the bitter end in the forts, which made up part of the Metaxas Line. We reported many heroic deeds by the defenders of the forts. I have a cutting from "The Times" dated Tuesday 8th April 1941. The passage of time has yellowed the paper, but amazingly it is still intact after spending 58 years in my diary!

A New Thermopylae

"How a handful of Greeks held up the main

German attack in the Rupel Pass, one of the most important sectors of the Greco-Bulgarian front, for 36 hours is told in a Reuters message from Athens. As soon as the full weight of the attack had been launched the Greek general called for volunteers to form an advance party and hold the line at all costs, while the main body took up their prearranged positions in the rear. Every one volunteered for this "regiment of death." A corporal selected 150 men. Holy Mass was performed on the battlefield after which the men started off on their first dangerous task of blowing up the bridges. In accomplishing this they destroyed many enemy tanks.

Then grimly, with the greatest bravery, they held on to their advance positions against tremendous odds. Soon they were outnumbered by 20 to one; but not until every man had been wiped out were the Germans able to pass."

On the next page of the diary there are items, which clearly demonstrate that, no matter how brave and determined the Greeks are, they cannot stem the overwhelming numbers of the advancing Germans. On the 9th April one armoured division outflanks the Greek defences and quickly captured Salonica. Dino Gregory and Constantinidis, who know Salonica well, are very distraught. They walk up and down uttering various in-

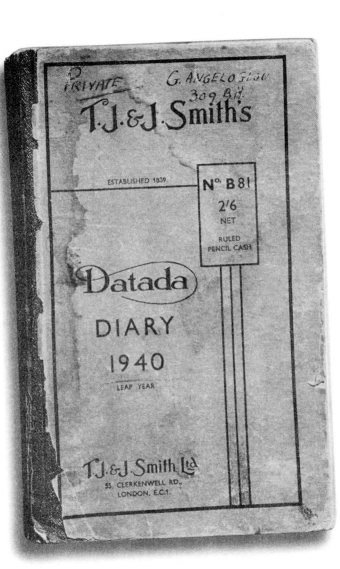

sults. "The beautiful Salonica has gone; the bloody Germans are going to eat up Salonica as they will eat up all those wonderful Baklavathes kai Tis Touloubes!"

On the same page of the diary there is an entry about the new air attacks on London, which began three days ago. The last thing we wanted on top of all the devastating news and our low spirits is to have more bombs. And the new raids are much more powerful than those of last year. And they last for about eight hours each! The one on the 16th and the other on the 19th were the heaviest raids that London has had so far - much damage and heavy casualties. God be with us!

Sunday 20th April ... This is our Easter Sunday. The worst Easter Sunday I remember. We all look worn out. Thank goodness we have two excellent talks about Easter. One by Archbishop Germanos - that charming intellectual Archbishop who writes and delivers his talks so well. The second talk is by Canon Douglas who speaks reasonably good Greek. But our Easter Day transmission is all serious and sorrowful. No-one is lively in the Section. How can you be, with four hours sleep a night!

After the midday transmission, however, things suddenly begin to change. It's just 2.30 pm when Basil Constantinidis and his wife turn up with a portable gramophone, a dozen Greek records and a basketful of luscious red eggs. They hand everyone an egg saying

"Christ is risen - Elate pedia, "Christos Anesti". They kiss everybody and start cracking eggs, first with Mary Moschona and Kali Jenks. Everyone joins in. Tony Mitsidis has the toughest egg and with it he demolishes all ours. We all laugh happily.

"POU TO VALES TO AVGO SOU,
VRE ANDONI! MESSA SE TSIMENTO?"

I stood back and looked at everyone. In a few minutes the Greek Section had been transformed. It was now a room full of excited laughing people. Then Basil puts on a record. It's a Kalamatianos. "XEKINA MIA PSA-ROPOULA." They all shout with pleasure as the pulsing rhythm of the Kalamatianos stirs them up. To the joy of everyone, Basil produces a large white handkerchief and starts to lead the dance. The door of the Section suddenly opens. All our neighbours are there, laughing and beating the rhythm with their hands and feet. Even our dour Albanian neighbour, Zavalani, is there and wants to join in the dance. When the record ends everyone breaks into a loud applause and shouts of "Christ is risen - Zeto e Ellas". Even Soteriadis is now drunk with the music. He shouts "Kalo Pasha pedia. Afto ene to Pasha tou Theou". The response is tremendous.

About an hour later things calm down. Work has got to be done. The next transmission is at 7.30 pm. Faces become somber again, sad. We don't broadcast any good news nowadays. It's all sorrowful news. These are

General Ian Jacob presents awards for broadcasting at the British Embassy in Athens.
<u>*From the right, nearest the camera, is*</u> *Dimitris Svolopoulos (Director General of Athens Radio), Tangie Lean (BBC director of European Services) and George Angeloglou.*

the last few days of FREE ATHENS. Poor Korizis, the new P.M., couldn't take it anymore. Poor bugger. So he shot himself on Good Friday; the right day to do this. So let's have some more bombs on London to make it easier for us to broadcast the bad news. How else can we compensate? Deaths in Athens and deaths in London. Death reigns supreme at present. We won't be able to sleep tonight!

Monday 21st April 1941 - that is Easter Monday. British troops are reported to have withdrawn again to a new line of defence. Germans have taken Volos and Lamia. Tsouderos, the banker, becomes Prime Minister. On the telephone Caclamanos tells me that "bankers don't make good politicians". "Hope he's a strong personality" he adds. It's 11 o'clock at night. Strangely no raid on London. Something to be grateful for!

Tuesday 22nd April 1941. A really mournful day. The gallant army of Epiros sign an Armistice at 4 p.m. No, it's a capitulation to the Germans, says the news, and later to the Italians. The Germans have given away to please Musso! Stupid Tsolakoglou signs the famous document. This is the bitter end to the victories, which had almost annihilated Mussolini's armies since last November. This terrible news and the bombs on London wear out our vitality and make working extremely slow. Even Maria is struggling to keep awake. Her typing is full of errors. But the bad news goes on and so does the war!

Wednesday 23rd April 1941. It was my name day. We announce that King George, his family and Cabinet leave Athens for Crete. This means they will have to cross the White Mountains and make their way right across Crete to the coast in the area of Sfakia. It's tough. Hope they make it! Perhaps St George will guard them. Soteriadis suddenly remembers "Chro polla vre Giorgo". I smiled cynically. "Na mas Zissis".

We have now reached "the endless night in Athens". No-one sleeps in Athens. Neither do we in London. How can you sleep with headphones round your neck and butterflies in your stomach!

The next two days in the diary are blank. I suppose I was exhausted like all of us. Anxiety wears you out quicker than physical exertion.

Sunday 27th April 1941. We start listening in very early. We now work like automata. The translators have large black circles under their eyes. Moschona looks like a wax doll. She can't hear very well. Dino Gregory can't hear at all. How can he? He is asleep over the typewriter!

The teleprinter suddenly comes to life. Quickly, we all gather round. The text reads "German tanks are entering Athens. They came down Leoforos Kifissias at a few minutes before 9 am. The thin line of imperial troops, who were fighting desperately to give their comrades time to slip away, are brushed aside by the mechanised

109

advance. An hour later a German detachment goes to the Acropolis. Two German soldiers lower the Greek flag and hoist the Swastika. A great silence falls over the city. All windows and shutters are closed. Curtains are drawn. Doors are locked. The silence is now complete. The Germans seem to have entered a dead city." In the Greek Section two people are weeping silently; one is Maria, the other is Kali. The rest of us are just dumb! Or rather, numb.

Suddenly Soteriadis bursts out "SKATA, SKATA. NA FATE NAZISTHES". Then he quickly walks out of the Section and bangs the door hard. It sounds like a bomb explosion. The girls stop crying. This is the start of the long German occupation!

CHAPTER 17

THE ATHENS RADIO SIGNATURE TUNE

As it became obvious that the German invasion of Greece was now reaching its final phase - with the occupation of Athens and the eventual occupation of the Peloponnese and some of the islands - we began to think how we should react to the changes that were bound to happen to Athens Radio. Naturally we knew that Athens would soon begin broadcasting with new staff and new announcers. We had the example of Salonica Radio which, after being occupied by the Germans on the 9th April, had started broadcasting for the Germans on the 12th April.

Soteriadis had first put forward the idea of us "stealing" the Athens signature tune and adopting it as our own. In other words, we would start all our broadcasts with a few seconds of the tune and then say "This is London" plus the explanation that as from today London and not Athens will be speaking for Greece - the FREE GREECE. The entire Greek Section enthusiastically agreed that "We shall speak for Greece, who cannot at present speak for herself".

On the 21st April, I went, with Soteriadis and Mitsi-dis, to see the Greek Minister, Haralambos Simopou-los, at 51 Upper Brook Street. This is the building that subsequently became the Embassy of Greece when the representative of Greece was upgraded to the rank of an Ambassador.

We asked the Greek Ambassador if he would agree to do an official handover of the Athens signature tune to us, the Greek Section. Ambassador Simopoulos was more than happy to officiate.

The next evening the Ambassador came to our studio accompanied by his Counsellor and his First Secretary. Also present were the Director General of the BBC, Sir Frederick Ogilvie, and the Director of Broadcasting of the European Service, Noel Newsome. It was all very formal. At precisely 7.30 p.m. BST the recorded signature tune was broadcast for the first time from London. Thirty seconds later Soteriadis, the announcer, was saying "Edo Londino, Kalispera Sas" and the evening transmission was on the air with everyone in the studio trying to restrain the tears of happiness and pride. It was a great moment for us; this entrusting of the Athens signature tune to the Greek Section for the period when Greece was going to be subjugated by Hitler and his forces. And so from that date on until Sunday, 5th November 1944 - for 3 years-we began all our transmissions, varying from six to nine times a day, with the Athens Radio Signature Tune.

The signature tune was called "To Tsopanopoulo" - The Shepherd Boy. It is a haunting nostalgic melody played on a flute, accompanied by numerous sheep bells tinkling at various distances, so that you get the impression that the young shepherd is watching over his flock on a peaceful hillside of the Peloponnese.

I remember that the flute and sheep bells brought a bit of light relief to our overwrought minds and took us back to the leafy landscape of Arcadia. We certainly needed this light relief during the three and a half years when we broadcast so many tragic and appalling acts of war, as well as amazing deeds of human courage.

Then on the 5th November 1944, we assembled to return the signature tune to the National Broadcasting Organisation of Greece. We were again collected in another studio, larger and more modern and with a different Director General and a different Greek Ambassador. The Director General of the BBC in 1944 was Sir William Haley, that distinguished newspaper editor - of both the Manchester Guardian and The Times - and the new Greek Ambassador, was Athanassios Agnidis.

William Haley opened the proceedings with these words:

"Your Excellency, we of the BBC were very proud when your predecessor, acting on behalf of the Athens Radio and the Greek people, gave into our safe keeping the Athens signature tune. We regarded it not only as

113

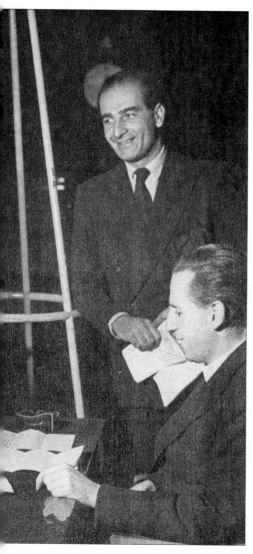

The BBC hands the Radio Athens call sign back to the Greek people.

Left to right: Mr. Callinicos, BBC Greek announcer, H. E. The Greek Ambassador to London M. Th. Aghnides, Mr. Noel Paton, Editor, BBC Greek Section, Mr. Capernaros, BBC Greek announcer, and Mr. W. J. Haley, Director-General of the BBC. In a ceremony broadcast in the evening Greek programme of the BBC European Service, on November 5th, 1944, the Director-General of the BBC handed back to H.E. The Greek Ambassador to London the call sigh of Radio Athens, to be used by a restored Greek broadcasting organisation. The call sign was entrusted to the BBC when Athens was occupied by the Germans in April, 1941.

a trust, but also as a symbol. For it was the symbol of the free voice of your very gallant nation."

"I now cordially welcome the opportunity of handing back to you the Athens signature tune, with the request that it may be conveyed to a restored Greek Broadcasting Organisation. I am very happy to assure your Excellency that we of the BBC will continue to do everything we can to nourish the deep friendship which exists between the peoples of Greece and Britain and in the work of broadcasting we look to a fruitful collaboration with your country."

The Greek Ambassador, Mr Agnidis, then replied:

"It is, Sir, with deep emotion that I have listened to your remarks and that I now receive back from you the Athens signature tune. In doing so I desire, in the name of my government, to express our sincere thanks to you and to all your associates who have cherished it in your safe-keeping.

Inevitably our thoughts go back to the dark days of 1941, and to the intervening years, during which the invaders of my country used the Athens Broadcasting Station as the channel of their calumnies and lies. Throughout that time the Call-Sign from London has stood as the symbol of truth and freedom, the symbol of a hope that could not be vanquished.

Today we witness the fulfilment of that hope, and the people of Greece will not forget that it was from these islands that the true voice of Greece was for so long broadcast to the world.

In this way the close ties of friendship between the British and the Greeks - ties that have been forged by common struggles, common suffering and common traditions - have been strengthened."

There was a loud spontaneous applause from the studio, which was followed by the playing of the two National Anthems. Everyone in the studio stood to attention. Our eyes were wet. It was the end of a great chapter in the history of the Greek Section. I shall always remember that night of the 5th November 1944, the night of the second freedom for Greece, the freedom of broadcasting.

Bush House, Aldwych, became the home of the Greek Section from the February 1941 and the headquarters of the BBC European Services.

CHAPTER 18

HAVING FUN WITH THE BOMBS

know this title seems ridiculous. But when you had
lived through those ten months of The Blitz, and
survived what was a very dangerous period, you
soon discovered that you also needed a sense of
humour, if not a sense of the ridiculous.

In the late Spring of 1941, when London was being
heavily bombed by the Luftwaffe, we often found that
after the last transmission at 10 pm (GMT) we could
not go home and we had to sleep the night in Bush
House. But one night there was a lull in the bombing
and Mimis Manolopoulos - another member of the Section - and I decided to go home by tube from Holborn
Station. Now the Holborn tube station was only a five
minute quick walk from Bush House, so we thought the
risk was small. We had our steel helmets on - we were
more frightened of shrapnel from London's anti-aircraft guns because the bits of steel that came down like
hail from the heavens were even more deadly than the
high explosive bombs.

We stood for a few minutes under the shelter of the solid arch of Bush House, and hearing nothing but distant flack fire, we decided to make a dash for it. But we had hardly covered a 100 yards when we suddenly heard the drone of what sounded like a whole squadron of German bombers. The fast moving criss-cross of the searchlights left us in no doubt that the bombers were coming fast and in one direction. We started to run up Kingsway, but the bombers soon caught up with us. Above the din of the ack-ack guns, we could hear the deadly fall-out of the shrapnel hitting the rooftops and the street.

Manolopoulos shouted at me, "Look for a doorway wide enough to give us some protection". We started running again not knowing where, but just looking frantically for any kind of shelter. Manolopoulos was shouting something above the shattering noise, which sounded like "My kingdom in Patras for a doorway".

Then the bombs came; pale and shaking we huddled against the metal door of a bank and counted the explosions. We knew that each aircraft dropped a stick of six bombs; one, two, three, four, - each one was spaced by about 100 yards and now the fifth was due to fall right on top of us. I shouted to Manolopoulos, " Get down and cover your face".

We both hit the pavement like a couple of well trained rugby players, only we were not tackling anyone. We heard the loud shrieking whistle of the falling fifth bomb, it sounded like a roaring express train - then there was an almighty explosion. The ground shook, buildings collapsed the debris and dust began to fall on us. One big piece of plaster hit Manolopoulos on his left shoulder and he thought it was a piece of shrapnel. "I've been hit," he shouted, "God, I shall probably die in Kingsway - of all places!" I raised my head and had a look at him. "Don't be a bloody fool", I said. "We are lucky. The bomb exploded behind this huge building, so we are OK."

With this reassurance, Manolopoulos got up and with a sprint that would not have shamed an Olympic runner, he made for Holborn tube station. I brought up the rear 50 yards behind him but I wasn't looking for medals that night, not even a bronze one.

Anyway, we didn't speak again until we had got into the bowels of the earth and on to the tube platform. Then Manolopoulos, miraculously recovered from the shock, began to laugh. "You should see your face, its covered in dirt and soaked in tar. You look a real clown". I had a sudden impulse to push him on to the live rail, but instead I too burst out into laughing. I think we both felt relieved to be alive as we looked at the mass of sleeping people on Platform 3 of Holborn tube station. A few minutes later, trying not to step on the occupants of the sleeping bags, we caught the last train for Queensway still marvelling at our amazing escape on Kingsway WC2.

A few years later the two of us again had another narrow escape, which, at least in retrospect, was equally funny. This time the incident took place on the Embankment, just outside the Temple tube station. The Allied invasion of Europe was progressing steadily but slowly. The Germans were still directing the flying bombs, or doodlebugs, towards London from bases in the Pas de Calais. Some 60 per cent of the flying bombs managed to get through the south coast defences and crashed in central London, often causing severe damage and serious casualties. On this particular day, 3rd July 1944, we had the longest flying bomb alert from 11.30 am to 8.30 pm. It was lunchtime, and as usual we went down to the Thames Embankment for some exercise.

There were four of us, but two went off to do some shopping and we continued our walk watching out for flying bombs. These V1s gave us one advantage over ordinary bombs; you could hear them and you could see them coming so you could take shelter. They were the prototype of modern guided missiles and resembled a miniature jet aircraft with very small wings. They carried almost a ton of high explosive and they flew at about 120 mph, at a height of only a few hundred feet, as they neared their target. At night especially, the flying bombs were a compelling sight. They looked like huge candles in the sky racing like fast and noisy motorbikes. When the engine of the V1 stopped - which meant it had used up all its fuel - the flying bomb went into a dive, hit the ground or a building and exploded. If you were in the open - within 400 yards of the impact - well, your number was up.

We had not reached the Temple Station gardens when we heard a V1 coming towards us over the Thames. Monolopoulos saw the V1 crossing the river at about 600 feet and heading straight for us. Without hesitating, he took a running dive into the ticket hall of the station while I huddled near a large metal bin used for collecting dead leaves from the gardens. But the jet engine didn't stop. It went on. We both got up and, fascinated by the 'motorbike of death', followed its course. Suddenly, the flying bomb did something completely unpredictable. It went into a sharp 180 degree turn and a few seconds later it was thundering back towards us, but this time barely at 300 feet. We held our breath as the bomb passed directly over our heads and we saw it re-cross the Thames heading for the south bank. It was losing height rapidly and a few moments later it crashed with a tremendous explosion on to the walls of a big warehouse. The explosion was so violent that it threw us to the ground and into a flowerbed. When we got up we were covered in daisies, dahlias and asters. Manolopoulos, ashen faced said, "The stupid bastards. They've got not only our names but our addresses as well".

Fortunately, a few days later, Montgomery captured the V1 launching sites in the Pas de Calais area in his offensive from the Seine to Antwerp. So we didn't have to become ex-directory!

CHAPTER 19

NOEL NEWSOME

I was the start of September 1941. Bush House was still untouched by bombs. I had just had a meeting with Noel Newsome, the Director of Broadcasts, and one of the most influential men in Bush House. Newsome was a jovial Yorkshireman with a fine journalistic reputation. He was a quick-witted, positive man who enjoyed having his way. He was also addicted to pipe smoking. A briar pipe was perpetually stuck in his mouth and quite often he had to use an air extractor to disperse the white clouds of 'Three Nuns' from his office. He loved salacious jokes. I was amused by the one about tobacco brands - both pipe and cigarette. It went like this. "He was only a tobacconist's son. But under a "Passing Cloud" and against the walls of "Three Castles" he shagged "Three Nuns" and was declared a "Players No. 1"!

Anyway, on that day, Newsome had told me that as from next week the Greek Section would have a sort of political supervisor, a member of the Political Intelligence Department of the Foreign Office. The person in question was Dilys Powell who was working as the film critic of the Sunday Times, knew Greece extremely well and was the widow of the well-known archaeologist and Philhellene, Humfry Payne.

I was a bit cautious in my reaction to this news but Newsome assured me that Miss Powell's position would actually be that of an adviser on British policy towards Greece, which he thought could be very useful. When I asked what sort of person Miss Powell was, he took his pipe out of his mouth and said "Intelligent, charming, very good looking and Oxford educated. That should suit you George", he added, taking again the briar out of his mouth. "And with a First in history and languages, and the looks of a film star. By jove, I'd be happy with that," he added with a mischievous grin. "Anyway, my boy, I'm afraid there is nothing we can do about P.I.D. You know there are too many departments chasing each other round the carousel of political propaganda and some of them stupidly try to challenge the authority of the BBC's European Service. But don't you worry, we've got them by the balls." He gave a happy derisory laugh and tried to relight the famous pipe.

Newsome was, of course, a great fighter and he had all the financial resources of the BBC. He had a superb staff and his policy of always telling the truth had brought the BBC immense prestige. All over Europe, then right through Africa to the far end of the Pacific, the voice of the BBC had become more or less sacrosanct. Lord Haw Haw had been ridiculed off the air, except when his broadcasts were listened to as a bit of a joke. For us Greeks, German propaganda was always sinister and we listened to it very carefully especially when we had news of shootings and executions of hostages. Every day there was a twenty to thirty page report on my desk of all enemy transmissions. It would take a couple of hours to go through this massive report from the "Monitoring Service", a superb service of the BBC which kept track of all enemy broadcasts. You got to know what Hitler was thinking and perhaps preparing to do. "The battle of the air", as we called it, was incessant, violent and very effective. So far we were winning it. But this was only the battle of words and we all knew that sometime, sooner or later, we had to destroy the voice of Hitler for good. And Newsome knew this better than most!

CHAPTER 20

THE BLONDE FROM THE FOREIGN OFFICE

The next day, I called a meeting of the whole Section. Some were irritated for being called in on their day off. One of them in fact phoned and asked if he could be excused. So I told him there was a rumour that we might go back to Evesham! He arrived in ten minutes flat!

When they all arrived, bursting with anxiety, I told them about Dilys Powell and the kind of functions she would perform, and that she had an office in the centre block of Bush House. There were a couple of disapproving murmurs, one loud cough and one despairing voice - that of Manolopoulos grunting - "For goodness sake, not a WOMAN to guide us through the labyrinth of Greek politics?" Silence followed as people moved nervously in their chairs. Suddenly, Soteriadis said, "Well boys, let's leave the anti-feminist of Patras out of this! But seriously, it might be easier to have a female gauleiter especially if she is a good looking woman", he laughingly added. Anyway, the meeting finished in great anxiety as most of the Section were not convinced that the Greek Section needed another "overseer".

Two days later, I invited Dilys to meet all members of the Section. Their reaction then was quite different. Dilys appeared beautifully coiffured and wearing a striking two-piece black suit with a white blouse. With her beautiful blonde hair, she was quite impressive and her soft shy smile denoted anything but a hard arrogant sexless nature. I noticed that she captivated all the Greek men. One or two thought it would be nice to take a woman like that out to dinner, even if only a meagre 5/- dinner. Meantime, the uninhibited Hector Tembros was mentally undressing her, with a lecherous smile on his face that betrayed his complete satisfaction with what he presumed he saw!

Dilys talked rather shyly at first, but when Greek words started cropping up in the conversation, she became more ebullient and started talking about the beauty spots of Greece that she knew so well, especially around the northern Peloponnese. The lively meeting lasted for about an hour, after which Dilys invited me to lunch at the Bush House restaurant in the central block. During lunch we discussed the strengths and weaknesses of each member of the Section. Dilys thought that I had a very intelligent and delightful Section and some very able secretaries. She was looking forward to working with us. We then talked about the impending arrival of the Greek

129

government in exile, which was due to arrive in London in September 1941, and the effect it would have on our broadcasts. She did not know any of Tsouderos's ministers and she had not yet met either the king or his brother. She was looking forward to working with all of them.

I looked at her pretty face and said to myself, "You are a very emotional woman and you will need all your intellect and strength when the Greek government arrives in England. I hope you will not fall victim to the great charm of the Greeks and the duplicity of the Greek political mind. One lovely romantic woman in love with Greece among a couple of dozen Greek wolves! I hope you will be able to keep your cool!"

Dilys Powell, of course, was leading a double life at that time. One life was devoted to the cinema and the Sunday Times and the other to being an Intelligence Officer in the Public Information Department. How did she manage this double life? Quite easily, it seemed. During the day Dilys worked in her P.I.D. office, but every so often she would slip out of Bush House and go and see a film. Then back to Bush House to finish her P.I.D. work. The cinema and films were never mentioned at the BBC. All her work for the Sunday Times was usually done at night in her own home. So the twain never met!

In the very beginning, very few people in the BBC knew that Dilys also worked for the Sunday Times. One day one of my announcers - a charming man with a sardonic sense of humour - spotted Dilys walking down the Strand. Out of curiosity, he followed her and suddenly saw Dilys disappear into the darkened entrance of the Tivoli Cinema. (This cinema disappeared in the late 1950s) Perplexed and curious, he went into the cinema and discovered that a John Wayne film was being screened, but only for film critics.

He came back to Bush House and straight into my office. "Did you know", he said ironically, "that Miss P-owell spends much of her time seeing films instead of informing us about British policy towards Greece? Do you think this is right?" Of course I knew all about Dilys's other work and I tried to convince my announcer by saying that this was obviously in her P.I.D. contract. "So she is being paid for this work! I see", he snorted. "So Miss Dilys Powell leads a double life! I wouldn't mind so much", he added, "if the films she saw were about Greece. But not this ghastly American cowboy and Red Indian trash. That's kids stuff, not political intelligence!"

Despite my announcer's objections, also shared by one or two others, this double life of Dilys Powell continued without interruption until 1946. Later, when the Greek government was established for a time in London, her life became complicated and occasionally extremely difficult. I think that then she found films, especially Westerns, a tremendous relaxation from the constant fireworks of Greek politics!

▲ *The judges of the Greek Section Listener Research Competition broadcast the names of the winners. **Judges left to right:** Francis Noel-Baker MP, George Angeloglou and film critic Dilys Powell - with Gordon Fraser and members of the Greek Section.*

Dilys Powell, who worked with the Greek Section during the war years, with Gordon Fraser (left), Rev Dr Germanos and George Angeloglou, study correspondence from listeners ▼

CHAPTER 21

THE GREEK GOVERNMENT IN LONDON

The Tsouderos government, once established in Park Street by September 1941 naturally started to become an active political organisation and made itself accessible to the British and International news media, as well as to the British academic world. Prime Minister Tsouderos made a good choice by appointing Andreas Michalopoulos as his Minister for Information. Michalopoulos was a tall good-looking Greek, who had studied Law at Oxford and later became a barrister. The Greek government immediately gained many advantages. However, they were not so lucky with some of the other Government staff who later caused the Greek Section a great deal of trouble.

At first I got on quite well with Michalopoulos but unfortunately, because of his social and educational background, he tended to be a conceited snob who thought that he was the top man in the exiled government, and that the Greek Section had to bow to his demands. He expected to have a regular weekly twenty-

▲ *The Greek Section studio during transmission*

A visit to the studios of Athens Radio ▼

minute commentary, which of course was absurd in a half hour transmission. At any rate we already had Caclamanos as our regular commentator, who incidentally did not think much of the Greek government itself because, apart from the King, none of the ministers in London had been elected by the people. In moments of light relief, Caclamanos, who had an acid wit when crossed, referred to the Tsouderos government as "the government of parachutists".

The other problem was that Michalopoulos expected that he would have the last word in matters affecting Greek affairs, whereas the policy in Bush House was dictated mostly by the progress of the war. We had many arguments on such matters in which Dilys Powell was involved. Dilys often said that Greece, like all the other allied governments in London, enjoyed the same freedom and was bound by the same restrictions in their broadcasting. This rule at first angered Michalopoulos, who thought it was belittling to classify Greece in the same category as countries like Belgium and Holland. Greece, he said, had almost annihilated the whole Italian army in six months in Albania, whereas Belgium and Holland more or less gave up the ghost the moment they heard the noise of the German stukas!

But I must admit that Michalopoulos, with the very valuable contacts that he had established, often achieved extremely good positive projection for Greece. Among the big meetings that he organised was the successful Anglo Hellenic League meeting - with the Duke of Kent as President. But perhaps the most remarkable tribute to Greece was the award to King George of the Honorary Doctorate from Cambridge University. This splendid occasion took place in the Cambridge Senate House and was attended by Stanley Baldwin, who was then the Chancellor of the University. After the Doctorate ceremony, there was a unique service in English and Greek in King's College Chapel. This was conducted by the Bishop of Lincoln and Archbishop Germanos, and attended by Winston Churchill. The event attracted tremendous interest and provided excellent coverage for the press and radio.

We, in the Greek Service, covered all these events very professionally with some excellent recordings in both the Senate House and during the service in King's College Chapel. George Megarefs, Panos Callinicos and Vrassidas Capernaros provided excellent linking material, which demonstrated once again how expert they had become in reporting important events. Michalopoulos, once again, was full of praise for us, which I think showed that he had a good sense of proportion. He knew that we were by now thoroughly expert in the presentation and analysis of public events, just as he recognised that most of our announcers had developed an attractive timbre in their voices.

CHAPTER 22

IVONE KIRKPATRICK

On the 23rd February 1942 Ivone Kirkpatrick's secretary rang me to say that Kirkpatrick wanted to see me on a personal matter as soon as possible. We agreed that I would call on the Controller of the European Service at 11 o'clock the next day.

Kirkpatrick was really a Foreign Office mandarin. An Oxford scholar with a First in French and German, he was appointed to the British Embassy in Berlin before the war. In 1941 he was seconded to the BBC and soon became the Controller of the European Service. After the war he was High Commissioner in Germany. He was also the person who interviewed Rudolph Hess in May 1941 when the German flew himself to Scotland in a fighter plane in the belief that he could persuade Britain to seek an honourable peace with Hitler. Hess remained, for the rest of his life, a frustrated and dejected prisoner, until he died in 1968.

Of course I knew what Kirkpatrick wanted to see me about. After all, for the last three months all sorts of ru-

mours had circulated around Bush House about myself
and the Greek Section. Fundamentally, it was a struggle
for supremacy between George Angeloglou, backed by
his announcers and the BBC, and the newly created
Greek Information Office under Andreas Michalopoulos. In a way it was a stupid conflict, because the BBC
would never give up control of its transmissions to a foreign government. The most the BBC would give would
be what we called some 'free time', as it had done in one
or two other cases. At the same time, the Greek Section
would not be allowed to become hostile in its broadcasts
about the Greek government. So therefore it was sense-
less to indulge in polemics with the Government in exile
in Park Street. In fact, I and my announcers although we
came from traditional Venizelist families, would never
allow ourselves to become Venizelist propagandists. At
any rate, this political dilemma would arise only after the
liberation of Greece when the Greek people would be
asked to decide the future of their political system. So, it
made little difference whether the Greek Section was
Venizelist or royalist as long as we did not embark on any
anti-royalist or anti-Tsouderos government propaganda,
which I can say truthfully we never did. But malicious
gossip was rampant and often created unfortunate mis-
understandings, even in the Greek Section itself.

Kirkpatrick, in the meantime, decided after considering various alternatives, that the only way to solve the

impasse between the Greek government, the BBC and myself was to appoint another person in my position - older, more mature, and of course English. Angelo-glou, he thought, though excellent in most ways, was too young and susceptible to various political influences and biases, both Greek and English. So, Kirkpatrick decided that a change of the head might calm spirits and give plenty of time for more sober thinking about this complicated and sensitive issue which threatened the peace and quiet of Bush House and certainly of the Greek Section.

Kirkpatrick, who knew me quite well, calculated that I would not resign and that after a period of hurt pride I would continue, as the second-in-command, to play a valuable part in the Section. "If I were you", Kirkpatrick went on to say, "I would not make too much fuss because you will only create opportunities for dissension and malicious gossip. Besides, as second in command you can exercise a lot of control on the Greek Section and its output."

I began to realise that Kirkpatrick was not really against me but he was taking a long line of resistance to the Greek government and especially King George's need and desire to remain King. I began to feel a little easier and to realise that I was involved in a subtle polit-ical game, obviously watched by Brendan Bracken and perhaps even by Churchill himself! So after being offered a cup of coffee and a biscuit, I was ushered out by Kirkpatrick, with a smile and the words "Try to be of good cheer, my boy. Things will work out to your advantage."

Next day, although still somewhat bruised and depressed, I went to see Caclamanos and I also managed to see Philip Noel Baker. Both of them thought that I had decided wisely to stay as number two in the Greek Section, and that I would still be able to exert considerable influence in the Greek Service and its programming. But some of my staff took it badly. Calinicos and Capernaros thought that this was a conspiracy led by King George and Tsouderos, aided and abetted by Dilys Powell! Soteriadis, more mature, looked further ahead. He said that it seemed that the BBC had now decided to back the right wing in Greece and that the return of King George was now more or less assured. But, he added, this would raise objections in and out of the House of Commons, which were against any serious British involvement in post-war Greek politics. For this reason, Soteriadis thought Kirkpatrick had now decided on my demotion to diffuse the antagonism against the Greek Section, which at any rate was ill-conceived and unwarranted. "It is up to you George," he said, "don't be disheartened. The Greek Section is bound to go through many more difficult and dramatic political periods before Greece is liberated, and afterwards, as

Greek politics mature and politicians become more responsible for their political ideas!"

I did not disagree, but feared some of the inevitable changes that would come about as the war went on, and especially when Greece was liberated. So it came about that Noel Paton was appointed as our Head of Section, a position he held for two years - after which I was reinstated.

CHAPTER 23

A LETTER FROM CAIRO

During the early 1940s I frequently received letters from my mother who lived in Egypt. They would arrive addressed to me personally, but c/o the British Broadcasting Corporation, London W1. Inside a light blue airmail envelope was a letter in Greek from my mother who knew little English, so the envelope was addressed by my father in his elegant handwriting. My father always enjoyed displaying his artistic skill in calligraphy to his business associates and especially to doctors, whom he considered had the worst handwriting when it came to the 25 letters of the Greek alphabet.

The most important items on the envelope were, of course, the Egyptian postage stamps. My mother would put on each envelope a variety of different values to please me as a stamp collector. At the time my favourites were the oblong airmail stamps issued in a set of 20 different values. The first cost One Milliem and the most expensive was 200 Milliem or £1. The attraction of this set of stamps was its design, which showed the three pyramids with a Hadley Page airliner of the 1930s just before it made a tight turn to land at the new Heliopolis aerodrome, a few miles from Cairo

The next important philatelic item was the light blue envelope, which was sealed with a long strip of gummed white paper, which was not put there by my mother. This was the mark of the Egyptian censor and the large blue capital letters declared that this envelope had been opened by censor. These three words of officialdom made the light blue envelope a very collectable item. I gently asked my mother if she could send me a few more such envelopes for other collectors in the BBC. Two of these fellow collectors did rather well from my mother's post - Mahmoud of the Arabic Section was one, and Lily, who was Assistant Head of the BBC's External Mail Service, was another avid stamp collector. Lily was always asking about my mother, who was always worrying about the inevitable attack on Egypt by Rommel which she, in common with many Egyptian Greeks, feared would bring about the end of the British administration in Egypt

The Greek Section was also worrying about Rommel but, unlike my mother, we knew that General Montgomery had been appointed Commander-in-Chief. Thus the El Alamein front had been strongly reinforced, not only with the latest American weapons, but also with

three highly experienced Corps Commanders - Lieute-
nant-Generals Horrocks, Lumsden and Leese. Horrocks
commanded three Free French brigades and the first
Greek Infantry brigade was commanded by Brigadier
Katsotas.

The now historical assault of the Eighth Army began
on October 23rd 1942 with a bombardment of 1000
guns, which continued for over 15 minutes taking the
Germans completely by surprise. The moment this barrage came to an end, having created havoc in the Africa
Corps and leaving great casualties, about 1200 tanks
went into action assisted by fighter aircraft of the Desert Airforce. The Germans were again taken by surprise but recovered sufficiently to engage in battle only to
be frustrated by very heavy rainstorms which continued
for two days, completely hampering both sides.

There were many changes of direction in the fighting.
What was decisive, of course, was the mastery of Montgomery who took advantage of every move of Rommel
until eventually the Eighth Army drove a wedge into the
enemy positions. Then suddenly a very skilful attack by
the 4th and 5th Indian division produced a complete
breakthrough. It was the end. The battle was won. It
could have been over earlier had desert storms not slowed down the Eighth Army's advance

In Cairo and Alexandria there was tremendous jubi-
lation. I heard later, in a letter from my father, how he

General Montgomery

and my mother were glued to their radio set and only took 15 minute breaks to have a cup of tea and munch a few of those lovely round Marie biscuits - which I had known so well as a small boy. Those days in late October and early November 1942 were unforgettable because while listening to the radio I was imagining that I was sitting at home in Cairo, in our favourite corner in the dining room, listening to the voices of Soteriades and Capernaros as they described the pursuit of the remnants of Rommel's fleeing defeated army which was now making its way towards Libya. Meanwhile, Italian Gene-

145

Ηλιούπολις 10 Ιουλίου 1942.

Αγαπημένι μου Γιώργο,

Ελάβαμε το Τηλεγράφημα σου εις το οποίον μας αναφέρης ότι έλαβες τας 300 λίρας και ότι έλαβες και το γράμμα μου και χαίρηκα πολύ που εσπλήξεις έλαβες ένα γράμμα μου εσπίλα αιπό τόσον καιρόν, σου γράφω και αυτό το γράμα ίσως και το λάβης και αυτό πιστεύω και η Ελένη να το έλαβε σας είχα γράψει και των δύο μαζύ ελπίζω και παρακαλώ νύχτα και ημέρα τον Θεόν να μας γλητώση αιπό αυτό το κακόν το οποίον αγε πρωτον μας μην τρωλάς τοις φόβοις μας και τας στεναχορίας που περνούμε εις αυτάς τας ημέρας ο αδελφός σου πρωτινλων αγε πόσο επίσημος ο Θεός να μας σώση και να βοηθήση τοις ιδικούς μας. πιστεύω να ασθε όλοι καλά και ο χριστοφόρος πιστεύω να εξακολουθή να πηγαίνη εις το σχολείον φαίνει σου να έχω ξέχκον να επήγαινε εις το σχολείον και να μην τον έχω ιδεί ακόμη αράγε θα με αξίωση ο Θεός να το φιλίσω αυτό το παιδάκη που το λαχταρώ τόσον πολύ; πόσον στεναχορούμε και δια την Ελένη που δε γένισε μόνη της χωρίς την μητέρα της ο Θεός να το βοηθήση το παιδάκι μου μόνον εις τον Θεόν έχω τας ελπίδας μου.

Το φαντίο σας αγε θαυμάσιο όλοι αγε ευχαριστημένη και τώρα αυτάς τας ημέρας οι αικούμε συγχολερα και παρηγορούμεθα εις αυτάς τας κακάς ημέρας που περνούμε

ἂν ἴδης τὴν Εἰρήνη νὰ τῆς εἰπῆς νὰ προσέχη τώρα πού εἶνε
εἰς αὐτὴν τὴν θέσιν νὰ μὴν τρέχη ἀπὸ ἐδῶ καὶ ἀπὸ ἐκεῖ
νὰ ἰσυχάση εἰς ἕνα μέρος, καὶ ἐζήτω νὰ μοῦ ὑπεγράφης
ὅπως εὐχάρισα πράγματα ἂν δὲν εἶνε δυνατὸν νὰ τὴν ἴδης
γράφεις, σᾶς ἔστησε χρήματα περισσότερα διότι δὲν ξεύρω-
με τί δὲν συμβῆ ὁ πατέρας ἤθελε νὰ σᾶς στήλη ἀκόμη
ἀλλὰ ἐζητήξαμε νὰ διορθωθοῦν τὰ πράγματα μὲ τὴν βοήθεια
τοῦ θεοῦ.   πολὺ φιλεῖ καὶ τὴν Πρίτα καὶ τὸν μικρόν μου
σὲ φιλῶ ἡ μητέρα σου

τοὺς νέους ἐκείνους δὲν τοὺς ξαναείδαμε πηόν ποῖος ξεύρη
τί γίνονται

rals were emerging all over the battlefield - not with weapons in their hands but suitcases of their clothes, walking to give themselves up, because the Germans had requisitioned all their transport. The cheers recorded for the Eighth Army when entering Ben-Ghazi were a moving tribute to the troops, and to Montgomery, who had turned out to be a magnificent leader.

Another letter from my Mother, carefully removed from its blue air mail envelope and dated mid-November 1942, was full of details about the approaching birth of a new grandchild - the battle of El Alamein had already now receded into the background. Eventually, in 1946 when I went to Cairo following the death of my Father, the reunion with my Mother was extremely moving. One of the things I wanted to see again in our house in Heliopolis was the powerful Phillips Radio on which my parents had always listened to the B.B.C Greek Service all through the war. The moment I saw the radio my Mother said: "My dear boy... this is the room we fought the war in. I don't think your Father would have survived the war without the help of the BBC's Greek broadcasts, and hearing your voice at the end of the evening transmission. The BBC was God - sent to us." - and she burst into tears. We sat for a long time holding hands in the dining room - I think we both felt much better after that.

CHAPTER 24

A SNAKE IN THE GRASS

The BBC Greek Section had some extraordinary ups and downs during the time I was its Director and for two years its Deputy Director. Naturally, the Greek Section lived through some extremely difficult periods and often the individuality of the Greeks clashed with the stubborn and often intolerant character of the British Civil Servant. On looking back over the years, I recall periods of which we are proud and occasionally I recall some events, which we would have preferred to forget. One particular incident cost me emotionally a great deal, but I suppose it also helped me to become a little more mature.

At the end of 1942 we had taken on a new translator announcer named Costas Hadjiargyris. He was very well educated and had a quick wit. He wanted to do commentaries, but I was against allowing a very new member of the Section the freedom which we only gave to older people like Soteriadis, who was a most experienced journalist from his time on the staff of several

Athens newspapers. Three members of my staff, Callinicos, Capernaros and Megarefs drew my attention to
the kind of language that this new staff member used,
which more experienced members of the Section considered Communist propaganda. At first it was easy to restrain Hadj - this is how Maria shortened his name - but
as he ingratiated himself with Noel Paton, our new
Head of Section, and often went out for a drink with
him, Hadj became more assertive within the Section.
We had several differences of opinion as to the language we used and one day an argument between
Capernaros and Hadjiargyris developed into a real KA-
VYAS - a shouting match.

I went into my office hoping that the two contestants
would calm down, when I suddenly heard Hadjiargyris
shout at Capernaros. "ESY EISAI ENA ZOON" ("You
are an animal"). The reply from Vrassidas was a right
swing to Hadj's jaw, which floored him. Mitsidis, who
was also there, rushed to get Hadj to his feet and at the
same time prevented Capernaros from delivering a second punch. I ran out from my office and shouted to
both the contestants, " For God's sake, have you two gone quite mad?" I was annoyed and so was Mitsidis.
Poor Maria was quite white in the face, but for once offered no tea to anyone. When things quietened down, I
took Capernaros into my office and he told me that Hadj
had been insulting him as they came up in the lift. The

argument was about the language and the style we used and Capernaros said to me once again that if we went the way Hadjiargyris wanted, the BBC Greek Section would soon be taken for a new Communist radio station.

The incident, however, did not finish there. Next day I went to see Dilys Powell and for the first time I was quite forceful with her about Hadjiargyris. I told her that she should ask for copies of all Hadjiargyris' commentaries. This she did and I remember how embarrassed she became after reading certain sections of his political commentaries. I thought that she was now obliged to do a full report for Kirkpatrick. In fact, for the next week or so I hardly saw Dilys. I assumed that the radio channels between London and Cairo must have been very busy.

Then about ten days later, Dilys asked to see me. She told me that I was quite right about Hadjiargyris and his language and that I was quite right that S.O.E and the Ambassador in Cairo had only one solution; his dismissal from the Greek Section. S.O.E. were very perturbed to see that censored news was being broadcast by the Greek Section itself. She showed me quite a few news items and a short commentary which contravened the regulations and which annoyed and angered the Cairo Ambassador, Rex Leeper, the S.O.E. and the Foreign Office. She also showed me two telegrams, which suggested that such flouting of the rules could not be tolerated in the BBC. Another telegram sent to Tsouderos showed the extent of the EAM penetration of Greek organisations abroad. At a meeting of Greek seamen in Cardiff it was urged not only that the Greek government should collaborate with EAM but that the Cardiff Greek seamen should be represented in the government. The two reports I read both ended with phrases like this:

"We feel very strongly that steps should be taken to remove Hadjiargyris from the BBC Greek Section before any further harm can be done."

Then a few days later Dilys phoned me and suggested that we meet in one of the offices of P.W.E. in Bush House. I agreed and we met just after lunch. Dilys started by saying that after going through a lot of material and talking to many people, she said that S.O.E. and the Ambassador in Cairo had only one solution, the dismissal of Hadjiargyris from the Greek Section. It was obvious that Dilys was now thinking along the same lines as I was, but that she was concerned over the possible repercussions in the Greek Section. I assured her that I did not think that any member of the Greek Section would be alarmed by the removal of Hadjiargyris, and that certainly the older members would, to say the least, be relieved at his departure. In fact, when the news that he was leaving the BBC was officially released a little while later, I had to restrain at least four of the Greek Section from bursting into a song and dancing in the corridors of Bush House.

After going through all these documents Dilys, who was by now quite nervously exhausted, changed the subject. She again wanted to know what effect the dismissal of Hadjiargyris would have on the other members of the Greek Section. I suddenly became light-hearted and said, "There is really one solution according to me, Dilys, and I think this solution will suit all parties, especially S.O.E. and Rex Leeper. I might even add that it will also suit people like Noel Paton. So let's have a look at Hadjiargyris' position. Costas, according to Greek law, was due for Greek military service and I know that the BBC had applied for his deferment, as we did for the few other young Greeks who had not done their military service before leaving Greece."

Dilys was now smiling and she looked quite relaxed. "Well George", she said. "Can I say that an idea like that crossed my mind some time ago but I thought I might have caused all sorts of other complications. But now that you have raised it, it seems the obvious thing to do. S.O.E., Rex Leeper and the Greek government will all be very pleased. In fact, I think one person will be more delighted than the others and that is Mr Tsouderos himself."

Once we talked to each other frankly and without fear that it might cause a revolution in Bush House, events moved very quickly. I can't quite remember all the details but I do remember that Hadjiargyris remained quite calm and in fact he seemed relieved.

This tragic chapter about Costas Hadj has a most unusual end. After that I didn't see Costas for several months, although I heard from various sources that he had taken part in the mutiny of the Greek navy in Alexandria. I do not know how Hadj participated in the mutiny except that, when it was quickly crushed, Hadj together with the other leaders was arrested, tried and imprisoned in a special camp set up in Bardia, Egypt.

I do not remember any details of his imprisonment, nor of his release, except that I later saw Hadj in Athens looking very much like he looked when we met in London as members of the Greek Section. Well, perhaps not so full of himself. I was in Athens for the BBC in the 1950s and I had an appointment to see the then Prime Minister, Sophoulis, whom I knew extremely well - he was from Samos - and we were distantly related on my mother's side. I got the shock of my life when I entered the Prime Minister's private office to be greeted by his personal Private Secretary, who was none other than Costas Hadjiargyris. Costas smiled at me and said, "The Prime Minister is waiting to see you." I made a supreme effort to keep myself under control, acknowledged him and went through the door to greet the Prime Minister. Sophoulis was as charming as ever - although he was not smoking his famous Dunhill pipe - and I had a very constructive interview, trying all the time to forget that Costas was the stepson of the Prime Minister Sophoulis! I suppose this could only happen in Greece.

The Most Reverend the Metropolitan of Thyateira, Doctor Germanos, broadcasting in the BBC's Greek Programme "You Ask Us - And We Answer"

155

CHAPTER 25

A FIGHTER PILOT FROM OVERSEAS

In the Autumn of 1942, when the survival of Britain was more or less decided by the fighter pilots of the RAF, I met a Canadian Greek fighter pilot called John Vassiliades. He came to Bush House to meet the Greek announcers, whom he admired for keeping up the morale of the suffering Greek people.

Vassiliades was born in Toronto of Greek parents from Sparta and who educated their three children to be bilingual. Their father thought that in this way Greek would never become a dead language.

When Italy attacked Greece in October 1940, Vassiliades Senior said to his son, "My boy, you will now go and fight for Greece if you can". Vassiliades Junior unfortunately could not go and fight in Greece, so instead he went and joined the RAF like so many other Canadians, Australians, New Zealanders and even Americans had done before America entered the war. Vassiliades trained for several months in Canada and was then transferred to Britain for further training.

After he got his wings, he joined a squadron stationed in South East England. By then John was an expert pilot and shortly afterwards he shot down two Messerschmitts over the Channel and was put up for a decoration.

The Greek Section, of course, was delighted to entertain Vassiliades and he loved talking Greek and about Greece. He did a wonderful interview with Capernaros, which reduced Maria Moschona to tears. One of the questions he was asked was how he felt during a dogfight. With a charming smile, Valliliades replied, "We never think about defeat. We are always on top because we are more experienced than the Germans - and we have the better aircraft. If you believe in yourself, the Spitfire will do wonders for you. You know, sometimes I feel sorry for the German pilots because we soon discover that most of them are not as good as we are. And don't forget the German pilots are operating from foreign bases, among people who hate them. This makes quite a difference you know!" And then, with a sensitive smile, he added in Greek "O theos einai mazi mas!" Maria Moschona, who was listening, bit her lip hard until it bled.

I saw Vassiliades once more and he told us that he was being transferred to the Midlands. Then I lost contact. In wartime this was quite common.

CHAPTER 26

THE FLYING FORTRESSES

One day in November 1942, I went to visit one of the aerodromes in England which had been taken over by the American Air Force. I did not know it, but as luck would have it, my arrival at the American air base coincided with the return of the American bombers from a big raid over occupied France. One hundred American Flying Fortresses had taken part in this raid on an important factory, now producing for the Germans. In fact it was the largest American raid carried out so far in Europe.

So you can imagine the excitement and tension of everyone at the base. We all watched the huge planes land on the tarmac one by one, and then be directed to a place on the perimeter of the field. Then the pilots and their crews clambered down from the planes and were taken in jeeps to the canteen, where they first had a cup of hot coffee or cocoa and something to eat. Then they went on to the Intelligence Unit for debriefing on the operation.

Afterwards I met some of the American pilots and their crews. Most of them were still too excited to want to sleep. They drank more hot drinks, ate buns and talked excitedly. You could see that they were happy by their faces. In fact they looked more like schoolboys who had won prizes after their exams than airmen who had carried out a large and successful operation against Germany.

One of them in particular was most exuberant. A short but stocky man - he was an ex-football player from the south - he cracked jokes in his broad, southern drawl while all the time his jaws chewed the inevitable gum. With his big shining eyes, out of proportion to the rest of his face, he radiated amiable self- confidence. I asked him how he got on. "Not too bad", he said, with a huge grin, "To tell you the truth buddy" he added, "I didn't make a fool of myself in this show like I did last time when I played football back home".

I spoke to other pilots, gun crews and navigators. One tall lanky airman was beaming from head to foot. He was one of the gunners and he had shot down a German fighter that had attacked them from below. "He came up at us", he went on, "at a terrific speed. I let him get quite near and then opened up on him, boy oh boy, you could see bits of his Messerschmitt flying all over the sky. He turned turtle and a few seconds later burst into flames and went in a spin." Yes, that lanky young gunner from Nebraska was really happy at that moment.

Then I noticed a rather quiet, unassuming airman who stood a little to one side. He looked young, very young in spite of his wool lined flying suit, which gave him an artificial paunch. Actually, he was just a boy. He told me, rather shyly, that this was his first operational flight and that he was a navigator on one of the Fortresses. I asked him how he felt. "A bit tired, but fine," he replied with a shy grin. "I had a funny feeling in the pit of my stomach before we took off, but the moment we were up it all went. You haven't much time to think then", he went on. "We got to our target on time, dropped our bombs and back we came. It was much easier than I thought. We saw German fighters but they never bothered us. That's all there was to it." He was silent for a moment and then, stretching his shoulders contentedly, he said "I can now go to sleep happy. I now know what it means to bring back your plane safely home".

He said all this in a quiet, understated way but I could feel his sense of satisfaction at having done a job well. That curly haired, shy American navigator was no longer a boy. He was now a man. After that, I went out to see some of the Flying Fortresses that had taken part in the raid. They all carried the names which their crews had given them. Peculiar names some of them; one was christened Stinky, another was Kentucky Moon, while another plane had the Skull and Crossbones on one side of the nose, and on the other the other side the words Hell's Battle Wagon.

When I left the base, I had seen and heard enough to know why these young American airmen had come to England. American youth, like that of the other Allied countries, had come to the fore to fight because their ideals had been challenged and threatened with extinction.

CHAPTER 27

A DOODLEBUG IN ALDWYCH

I t was just before one o'clock on Friday, 30th June 1944. The small popular Aldwych post office in the Bush House building facing Kingsway was, as usual, crowded with lunchtime shoppers, people buying stamps, weighing letters and parcels. I had just got back to our office on the third floor of the south-east wing when I suddenly heard the unmistakable motor bike noise of a flying bomb. In a few seconds, I said to myself, the motor will cut out and the explosion will shatter everything around us.

I instinctively fell to my knees while I shouted to Maria, who was typing a script a few feet away, "Take care of your eyes Maria, and don't move".

It was a huge explosion. Maria's own little tea service shattered into hundreds of tiny pieces and my ears went deaf. Maria got up and came over to me. "Are you alright Angie?" she asked. "Thank goodness only one of our windows smashed." I smiled and said "Quite a big bang. Maria, I think I shall go downstairs and see what the damage is. You stay here."

I tried to go down to the entrance hall. It was difficult as all entrances into Bush House were crowded with people and the police were trying to prevent more from entering the building. The area of Bush House that faced Kingsway was covered in debris, especially near the destroyed post office. Several ambulances were parked on the pavements and stretcher bearers were moving among the damage with difficulty. The worst sight was just in front of the main entrance to Bush House. There was a large wooden coal cart drawn by a big dray horse. The cart had lost three of its wheels and all the coal had emptied into the street. But there was no horse to be seen. Someone pointed to the small verandah on the first floor over the entrance to Bush House. I looked up and saw the most sickening sight of all. One black dray horse lying across the balustrade soaked in blood - but without its head. I winced and decided I'd had enough.

I made my way back to our office. Maria was still typing, but not at her usual speed. She looked pretty awful but amazingly she had a second small china teapot full of tea. She said nothing, but simply poured me a cup and put four lumps of sugar. "Two more lumps Angie today to help your blood pressure". I said "Maria, you would have been a very good nurse". She smiled and asked, "Is it really bad Angie?" "Yes", I said, "the worst I have seen so far."

Only one broken window, I thought but how many

lives lost as a result of that one bomb? The next day the papers told us. The Daily Express called the Aldwych bombing "The Aldwych massacre". They said that 52 people were killed on the spot and more than 200 were injured, some very seriously. The Express did not mention that one dray horse was decapitated!

The V1 flying bombs, or doodlebugs, started to fall on Greater London on the 12th June 1944. It was barely seven days after the Allied invasion of Normandy on the 6th June.

The V1 was a small, pilotless midwing monoplane, with a pointed nose that contained up to 1,000 kilos of high explosive. The V1s were launched from ramps in France, Belgium and Holland. The black devils, as we called them, once properly launched could travel at speeds of well over 460 mph which made them difficult targets for both anti aircraft guns and fighters.

The V1, although it worked as a weapon especially against the civilians, was nevertheless not 100 per cent effective. Fear it certainly instilled, especially in the first two months, but gradually this fear lessened and people even learnt how to avoid the doodlebugs. It did a great deal of damage to buildings, but then any weapon of the V1 type could do this. I personally thought that the V1 was less dangerous than the conventional bomb. The conventional bomb whistled as it came down and gave you only a few seconds to get into a shelter, whereas the doodlebug allowed you to see it and move out of its range.

During the time when V1s were being used, the doodlebug claimed a total of around 6,500 civilians killed and 14,900 severely injured.

Meantime, the Germans were successfully coping with the development of the V2, another and more serious weapon than the V1, which had been developed at Peenemunde on the Baltic Sea. The V2, larger, faster and more destructive, travelled at the speed of sound and itself was silent - until it exploded. The V2s were launched at the rate of 600 a month, usually from Antwerp or The Hague, which was only four minute's flight from London. About 500 succeeded in reaching the London area and caused great devastation when they hit their targets.

However, as Germany faced defeat the team in Peenemunde, now working on new projects, decided that the only course for von Braun and his colleagues would be to surrender. But Peenemunde was destined to be in the Russian zone and they wanted to surrender to the Americans. Eventually, four thousand employees - scientists and technicians - asked if they could move into the American sector. This was done and so von Braun gradually achieved his ambition. He was taken to America where he became Director of the Apollo Space Project, which would land the first man on the moon.

CHAPTER 28

A LIGHT HEARTED INTERLUDE

Throughout our working days at the BBC, even at the worst periods of the war, we always tried to keep our spirits up by appreciating the humour of certain small and amusing incidents. You needed a sense of humour and any incident, which produced a smile or raised a laugh, helped you get through the day. The following incident took place in the immediate post -war period - when food was still rationed.

I was sitting in my office reading a press review when my phone rang. It was a Greek gentleman who wanted to meet me. He came from a well-known Greek shipping family by the name of Louloudis, and he had been living in Bucharest until he managed to get out. Naturally, he spoke both Greek and Romanian. He was with a group of Greeks brought over by the British Council to see post- war Britain. He said he would like to do a talk about Greek life in the Romanian capital. I accepted and told him to write no more than fifteen hundred words, and to let me have his script a couple of days before the recording.

On the appointed day, he arrived as expected but with a script of five thousand words! In this case, cutting it down was not too difficult as a great part of the script was about the food the Greeks of Bucharest enjoyed before the war. When I made the cuts, we were left with a quite interesting talk about Greek life in pre-war Bucharest. When we finished the recording Louloudis said to me, "When do you have lunch in London?" I realised that the man was hungry and of course I had to take him out to lunch. I looked at his rotund waistline and decided that I had better take him to one of the three or four good Cypriot restaurants which served reasonable food and were willing, in certain cases, to overlook the legal five shilling meal! My guest looked as if he could devour not just a wing of a chicken, but an entire well-fed capon. So I took him to Louis; and the owner, gave us a good table and a carafe of Cypriot white wine.

The moment we sat down Louloudis continued his running commentary on the food delights of Bucharest. I ordered him a glass of ouzo. The food arrived. The first course was one Portuguese sardine, a slice of tomato and cucumber, and two olives! Mr Louloudis placed everything on his fork and gulped them down in one mouthful. I ordered him a second ouzo and said 'Yiassou'. He said "Is this the appetizer?" "Well yes", I replied, "we now have the main course." His face fell. He just said "oh". The second course consisted of two potatoes, some cauliflower and the wing of a chicken. The procedure was the same. In one gulp the chicken disappeared and the vegetables followed in another gulp. I began to perspire. I called Louis. He whispered in my ear that a food inspector was sitting not very far from our table and with a wink he disappeared. Meantime, Louloudis was getting agitated. He kept on saying, "When do we start lunch?" Perspiration was now dripping down my neck, which made me feel that my shirt collar was two sizes too small. I made up my mind and asked for the bill. It was ten shillings plus another ten shillings for the drinks. I paid quickly and told Louis that we were going to another restaurant.

Louloudis was famished. His tummy was rumbling. We more or less ran across Oxford Street into Wigmore Street, to my second restaurant called "Plato". The owner, another Cypriot, was always willing to stretch a rule for a friend. We sat down and I introduced the owner to Louloudis and the boss winked at me as if he understood what we wanted. Actually, this 5 shilling meal was more or less like that of Louis's except that the chicken was twice the size. However, this slightly larger portion had no effect on Louloudis' appetite. In fact, in about ten minutes, he had eaten both the first and second course and was now on his second glass of wine. After that he whispered to me that he was now ready for the main course! I thought it was time for us to leave, not only

Plato's, but London too. I paid the bill, got him in a taxi and we made our way to the third restaurant of my choice. This was in Soho, The Elysee restaurant was owned by a very dear man we used to call Mickey Mouse because of his diminutive size. As we entered, I whispered in his ear, "Is it all clear?" "The light is completely green" he replied with a smile. "Fine" I said, "In that case let's have two full meals and to hell with rationing."

Well, we did enjoy the Elysee. The food was good, the courses sizeable and the Cypriot wine was excellent. We even had two Greek coffees. Louloudis was at last in good spirits. He looked at his huge tummy and laughed. "As you see, the stomach is at peace at last", he said, and then without pausing he went on to describe the biggest meal he had ever had in Bucharest. One kilogram of beef, one kilogram of lamb and two kilograms of pork all cooked in a fantastic sauce and served on a huge mound of rice. I felt quite sick. I was also beginning to worry about the bills. Three bills on the same day, ouzo and wine and coffees, well that was quite a mess.

At about 3 o'clock, when I eventually got rid of my now unwelcome guest and went back to Bush House I went to see another producer and a good friend of mine. I told him the whole story. He burst into fits of laughter. He thought this was one of the funniest BBC hospitality meals he had ever heard. "Well" he finally said, "A bloody funny story but much of it is your fault George. You should have left Louloudis with the one sardine and two olives! But let's be serious; what are you worrying about? Your guest was part of a British Council group of foreign visitors to post-war Britain. Well, you could stretch a point and say you were entertaining three Greek visitors. After all the British Council is paying for their visits and you are asking the BBC to pay for three measly lunches. For goodness sake, don't be stupid. For more than three years the Greeks have paid with their blood in order to fight on the side of the Allies. So what's two or three quid for a meal by comparison?" he laughed. After that there was nothing more to be said.

CHAPTER 29

IN SEARCH OF A DEPUTY

"George, I think you need a second-in-command in the Greek Section", said Gordon Fraser to me in January 1947. "Your transmissions are getting more ambitious. You've got a civil war in Greece, a new Greek government and a large Greek audience overseas. I don't think you can do it by yourself. You need a responsible active deputy to take some of the burden off your hands." He laughed and added, "Besides, with so many lively and volatile Greeks you might find that a dry, phlegmatic Englishman will be a tonic for you".

Gordon Fraser was the head of the South East European Services which included, in those days, Greece. Gordon was an efficient cultured man of great charm who had been a Lieutenant Colonel in the Army. After being demobbed he was taken on by the BBC for a couple of years, at the end of which he would go back to his important printing business, which later produced some of the finest greetings cards on the market - and still does today.

Of course I did not disagree with Gordon because it had become quite obvious that I needed a reliable and knowledgeable deputy editor. So there was no need for further discussion. In a few weeks the necessary adverts were placed in the press and a little while later we received applications from nine Englishmen. Four of the candidates were unsuitable for various reasons, but the other five were invited for a Selection Board. To my great surprise, amongst these, was Lawrence Durrell. I did not know that Durrell was looking for a job. I thought he was still in Rhodes after spending four years in Cairo and Alexandria. Durrell, of course, was a gifted writer and poet.

There was also another very good candidate and that was Stanley Mayes. He stood out because he knew Greece and the Greek people extremely well, spoke reasonable Greek, and had spent a couple of years as liaison officer with the Zervas guerillas in north west Greece. The Board which would choose the best candidate from the five applicants consisted of the Appointments Officer; the Assistant Head of Administration; a representative of the Ministry of Information; Tangie Lean, Chief Deputy to the D.G, who at that time was Lieutenant General Sir Ian Jacob, and myself.

The first three candidates did reasonable interviews. Mayes did an excellent interview, and finally came the turn of Lawrence Durrell. At first Durrell seemed rather dull and not particularly interested in answering some of the questions put to him, but when I took over he became more interested and lively. My first question was, "why do you want to join the Greek Section of the BBC?" Durrell's eyes lit up and with a soft and rather emotive voice he said, "It's quite simple. When I first went to Corfu in 1935 I began to realise that England constricts the sensibilities of man, whereas Greece opens them out. I gradually fell in love with Greece and this love has endured for twelve years now in spite of many vicissitudes. I realised this especially when I went to Rhodes in 1946 as Public Information officer of the Dodecanese. It was good to feel alive again among people I could happily identify with. I think coming to work here in the Greek Section would suit me greatly. It would add zest to my life which I greatly need". He added, "Does this answer your question?"

It certainly did. I knew that Durrell was streets above the others and I was already visualising the imaginative programmes we could do with him. So after that, I took no interest in the other questions. As far as I was concerned, there was nothing more I wanted to hear. But the Board disagreed with me. I argued all my points, but the other four members were unconvinced. All four of them plugged for Stanley Mayes. At one time I lost my temper and naively said, "After all, the man we choose has got to work with me and not with you!" There were several frowns and one cough but no-one said anything. We had reached a complete impasse.

The Appointments Officer offered more cups of tea. I kept a grim silence. Suddenly Tangie Lean got up and came over to me. He suggested we had a chat at the other end of the large Boardroom. We did. Tangie said "George, I want you to think deeply for a moment. Lawrence Durrell is a first class man, I like his prose and his poetry but I don't think he will be good as your number two. That's what it's all about; a good number two, not a brilliant writer or poet. Durrell is too much of an individual, self indulgent and conscious of his talent. But can he go up and down to the studio, checking scripts, cutting and editing and keeping your staff in order? These are all mundane chores. Besides, he has the reputation of being a heavy drinker and a great womaniser. So in a little while, he'll start going out a lot, meeting interesting people and spending less time in Bush House. We all think that Stanley Mayes is a better man for the job. Yes, just for this particular job we think that Mayes is the better candidate. So please don't prolong this Board meeting!"

I was a little taken aback, but I also realised that if I insisted on Durrell I would be outvoted four to one. Anyway Tangie was an experienced and fair-minded person. He was also a good friend and also, at the same time, my boss. So we had a third cup of tea and then went back to our chairs. I think the rest of the Board knew that Tangie had convinced me. But deep down, I also knew that something else had influenced their decision. I thought with a smile, "Two lovers of Greece, not to mention Cyprus, might cause too many storms in the Greek Section!"

So the letters went out to the candidates and Lawrence Durrell was obviously very peeved. He went back to Bournemouth, the family home, and a little while later he was sent off as Director of the British Council Institute in Cordoba, Argentina where he spent just over a year. He was bored with the job but wrote three excellent humorous books about the British Diplomatic Service. After that he went to Cyprus for two very eventful years. They were certainly not boring!

Meantime, Stanley Mayes turned out to be an able second-in-command. He was very much in touch with Greek affairs and he learnt how to cope with the frailties of the Greek character and the intricacies of Greek politics. At first the Section was a little reluctant, but eventually they decided that Stanley Mayes was a real English gentleman. A good journalist and writer, Stanley turned out to be an excellent and loyal number two, who gave me his unstinting support in the running of the Section, and in moments of crisis stood by me even though we were to disagree on the subject of Cyprus. We always remained good friends.

Nevertheless, I often wonder whether by refusing to take on Lawrence Durrell in the Greek Section we did him a great service and perhaps contributed towards his incentive to write the Alexandria Quartet. On the other hand, maybe the BBC lost out, because it is quite possible that Durrell might have written a four-book saga about the BBC, with perhaps the title "The Ariel Quartet"! Who knows?

CHAPTER 30

KENNETH MATTHEWS

first met Kenneth Matthews at the start of 1940. He was then a producer in the BBC Transcription Service. He used to come to Bush House to see us and to talk a little Greek. His modern Greek was good as he had studied Ancient Greek and Philosophy at Cambridge, travelled extensively in Greece during the vacations, and finally spent two years at the elite Greek boarding school on Spetses, teaching English to the privileged sons of the Athenian upper classes. Kenneth was a soft spoken, humorous man and his English accent only added further attraction to his sensitive romantic nature.

I got on very well with Kenneth and we ate together in the Bush House canteen and talked about old days in Greece and the great number of charming young women he had met in Athens during his Spetses school holidays. The paradox was that although Kenneth was physically not a very striking man - he was almost bald at the age of 30 - he always attracted women, especially younger women.

Some time in 1940 Kenneth Matthews decided to move into news and he was appointed as Middle East and Balkan correspondent of the BBC, based in Cairo. He did excellent work especially during the Cairo and Teheran conferences. But Kenneth really came into his element as a correspondent after the war, when he became deeply involved in the Greek Communist rebellions and later in the long Civil War. No other foreign correspondent knew the character and temperament of the Greeks better than he and his distress became apparent when he saw the weaknesses, follies and tragedies of the Civil War period. At this time he wrote some special reports for the Greek Service which were so dramatic that the announcer reading them was moved to tears. These reports told of the appalling blind violence of the Civil War and helped us to keep our sense of proportion, when we were attacked by some British left wing commentators and by certain British academics, who considered that Greece should have been given up to the freedom of communism.

I remember a heart-rending report, which Kenneth sent us about the retreating guerrillas after the cease-fire in Athens in 1945.

"When defeat stared them in the face," said Kenneth, "the Communists began to take hostages. They took people from their homes and marched them into the interior, men and women, rich and

*poor, young and old, dragooned into wretched strag-
gling columns and driven like cattle for up to ten
hours at a stretch over the country roads and snow
covered passes. Many were shot or bayoneted to
death because they could not keep up; many died of
exposure. Perhaps twenty thousand civilians were
abducted in this way, adding to the thousand British
prisoners-of-war who were similarly treated. Something like a moan of anguish rose from the city as
the stories trickled back and family after family recorded its victims."*

Kenneth continued to cover the civil war until 1949
and quotations from his despatches appeared in newspapers and on the radio all over the world.

In October 1948, however, by some strange twist of
fate, Kenneth Matthews was captured by the Communist guerrillas and held prisoner for ten days. Now all
this would not have happened had Kenneth been less
susceptible to the charms of women. In those days he
knew a very attractive young woman called Anna Michael, who also worked for the BBC. Anna was Jewish,
half Polish and half Austrian, and Kenneth became very
attached to her. She had never been to Greece so she
asked Kenneth if he would show her around Athens.
Kenneth then had the romantic idea of taking Anna
down to see Mycenae and the famous city of Agame-
mnon. This was a rather dangerous trip as some two

thirds of the Peloponnese was held by, or riddled with, the Ellas guerrillas. Anyway, heeding no warning, they decided to spend the night in the simple but most celebrated inn, La Belle Helene, as it was known since the first edition of Baedeker. Unfortunately for Kenneth and Anna their romantic idyll was very short lived. Half an hour after getting to their room there was a knock on the door and a gun was thrust in the face of Kenneth by a dark handsome young man, who ordered them to come down to the ground floor. Kenneth protested saying that he could not leave because his girlfriend was a complete stranger to Greece. At any rate, after much arguing and after receiving his orders from headquarters, the local guerrilla leader said that Anna could stay behind in Mycenae. Eventually, Kenneth and his abductors departed and Anna was left in the solitude of the Mycenaean love nest.

What happened afterwards was a long story which was reported extensively both in the Greek and international press.

Kenneth was marched up and down, sometimes on horseback, the mountain paths and valleys of Eriman-thos and saw a great deal of life in the guerrilla occupied areas. He was exhausted, not so much from fearing for his own life as from the rigours of the climbing and marching, especially after dark. We were all very anxious about his safety, with the fate of George Polk still uppermost in our minds. A year earlier George Polk, the Columbian Broadcasting correspondent in Athens, had gone to Salonica to try and interview some of the guerrilla leaders. He never got the interviews because he was killed and his trussed-up body was found floating in the Bay of Salonica. "It was an execution and a political demonstration," said one of the papers. I remember receiving a telephone call from Anna from the Greek Embassy in Athens and she was almost hysterical about Kenneth's safety. "I am scared" she said, "he is not going to survive. He'll be another George Polk." I tried to reason with her saying that Kenneth Matthews was a different man and at any rate he was the BBC correspondent, which I thought would surely count for something.

I also remember the great arguments we had in the Greek Section about Kenneth's ultimate fate. Every day, after the evening transmission, we all gave vent to our feelings by imagining what could happen to Matthews. Most of the Section was despondent but Soteriadis and I were optimists. "Nonsense", Soteriadis kept on saying, "there is no comparison between Matthews and George Polk. Nobody knows who murdered Polk but everyone knows that Matthews is held by ELLAS. So if they kill him, public opinion will turn violently against them, which is the last thing ELLAS wants. All they want from Matthews is some good reporting of how well they govern the areas they occupy - the new Greece, as they call it. A dead body is no good to them. So I'll take you a bet", he added with a cynical smile, "a gold sovereign if you like, that very soon Matthews will be set free and he'll be back sending despatches about his stay with the guerillas!"

There was a hush, but no bets were taken. Only Manolopoulos said scathingly, "It's all very well. But can you trust the buggers?"

Soteriadis was right. Nothing happened to Kenneth. He toured a number of villages held by the guerrillas and was shown the way they administered them. On the whole he was treated extremely well. I really think it was the kudos of the BBC and the expectation of maximum publicity for ELLAS that kept Kenneth very much alive. Also, there was another good reason. In the days of relative peace in 1946, Kenneth had met the editor of the main Communist newspaper, Rizospastis - the up-rooter - called Costas Karageorgis, known to foreign correspondents as Black George. This ex-editor had now become one of the leaders of the Ellas forces in northern Greece and he obviously interceded on behalf of Matthews and suggested that he should be given all the freedom to report the amazing improvement of life in the Ellas occupied areas.

Eventually, on the orders of Black George, Kenneth was set free in the suburbs of Patras. He was then taken to Athens by the police, where he was extensively ques-

The Greek Section's daily programme conference. George Angeloglou is seen in the centre with Stanley Mayes (his deputy) on his left.

tioned by Greek and British Intelligence. Here he was also reunited with Anna, who was by then very stressed out, and they were brought back to London for the final debriefing. Unfortunately, the BBC did not treat the abduction as a reportage scoop. General Jacob, the D.G. - a military man himself - saw the whole affair as dangerous and disgraceful. George Barnes, Director of the Spoken Word, accused Kenneth of lack of responsibility and loyalty. He was not allowed to broadcast anything about his abduction. As a penalty, he was banished in disgrace to what journalists called "the graveyard", the department which writes obituary notices in advance for those who are expected to die. This was indeed a very hard sentence to pass on a man like Kenneth Matthews, who had brilliantly covered the Greek Civil War, and whose reports had been universally admired and quoted in newspapers and magazines the world over.

Unfortunately, because of his demotion, Kenneth was deprived of the excitement of reporting the end of the communist insurrection. This came in the summer of 1949 and happened because of three things. The strength and spirit of the Greek army now equipped with the latest American weapons; the withdrawal of Tito's support and the closing of the Yugoslav-Greek frontier in July that year; and the sudden, eccentric change in the command of the Communist forces as-

George Seferis, the distinguished Greek poet, broadcasting in the
BBC Greek Service on 7th July, when he paid a personal tribute
to Greece's great lyric poet, Angelos Sikelianos, who died in
Athens on 20th June, 1951.
George Seferis, later became a Counsellor at the Greek Embassy
in London.

sumed by Zachariadis, the Secretary General of the KKE. The result was that in December 1948, the new Communist Commander-in-Chief suffered several defeats. One of the bloodiest was at Florina where he lost more than twelve hundred men in one attack. The final offensive by the army started in August and by the end of the month, the communists were fleeing across the frontiers.

Poor Kenneth watched and heard the dramatic denouement of the Civil War from the distant shelter of an office in the basement of Broadcasting House. He was disconsolate. Of course Kenneth Matthews was later forgiven, and he held various jobs as a foreign affairs commentator in television news. Finally, he became News Editor in Norwich, one of the BBC's regional offices. But Kenneth was hurt and disillusioned with the BBC. When I met him just before he went to Norwich, he looked completely out of sorts. We talked a little about Greece, the past and his dismissal. "My dear Kenneth", I suddenly said, "you, with all your experience and wisdom, don't you know that the British establishment never forgives you once you dare to cross it?" Kenneth laughed, but made no reply.

CHAPTER 31

THE GOLDEN YEARS OF THE
GREEK SECTION

This period began about the start of 1945 and came to a tragic end in 1957-8. I call it "golden" because these were very happy and productive years when the Greek Section produced many imaginative programmes, the announcers developed their own idiosyncratic styles, and we set new standards in both the spoken word and in the presentation of talks and features. News reading achieved a lively rhythmic pace, the voice was smooth and controlled and enunciation was rounded and clear. Anyone who compared our pace and diction with that of the Athens Radio speakers immediately noted the mature professionalism of London. I remember the valuable services given to the Greek Section after the war by people like George Pastelidis, Nanos Valaoritis, Zissimos Lorentzatos, Paul Stassinos, Spyros Babouris and Mihalis Stylianou.

This was also the period when hundreds of Greeks visiting Britain, either as guests of the British Council

The Greek Section on air: (Left to right) Dimitris Horn, Nanos Valaoritis, Zisimos Lorentzatos, Panos Callinicos and Apostolos Sahinis

188

or on their own initiative, would be invited to visit Bush House. So the Greek Section, as well as the Cypriot Section, which was housed in Oxford Street under Michael Cacoyannis, became a kind of social club where Greeks came to talk Greek and enjoy the friendly atmosphere of EDO LONDINO.

Among the guests who came to Bush House were many of Greece's distinguished writers, politicians, actors, musicians and men of science. I need only to mention a few at random in order to explain the great attraction the Greek Section had for those who came to visit London. Amongst them were Nikos Kazantzakis, Katina Paxinou, Alexis Minotis, Takis Horn, Gina Bachauer, Archbishop Damaskinos, Panayotis Pipinelis, Manolis Kalomiris, Mikis Theodorakis, Manos Hadjidakis, Sophia Vembo, Maria Callas, and George Seferis. In addition to every well known Greek journalist we saw a number of distinguished military leaders like Bernard Freyberg, Jumbo Wilson, Wavell, Montgomery and Alexander. And there were many others, who were either visiting London or who were looking for an opening in England. London was the new capital of Europe, and although badly scarred and short of most things, was hugely admired by all those who had suffered under the German occupation.

And, in the Greek Section, we were delighted and honoured to put on the air all these talented men and women, who were linked in one way or another with the new Greece, that was struggling to survive the

189

hard conditions of the post war era, after the destruction brought by the Civil War. Political parties were not yet strong enough and petty political jealousies and mistrust prevented the formation of a strong coalition for many months, until Field Marshal Papagos resigned from the Army and entered politics. In the subsequent elections he swept the board and created the Greek Rally Party. And although these thirteen years between 1945 and 1958 were not exactly easy for us, they were nevertheless the best years of our life in broadcasting to Greece and to the Greeks overseas.

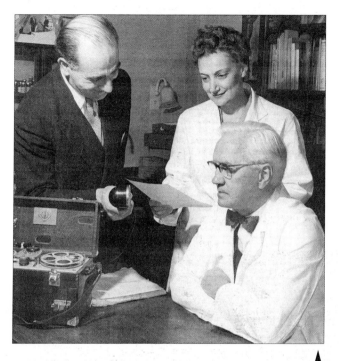

Sir Alexander and Lady Fleming were interviewd by Vrasidas
Capernaros, BBC Greek Service, on the occasion of the Centenary of St. Mary's Hospital Medical School, London. A talk on
the Centenary of the Medical School was broadcoast in the BBC
Greek Service on 9th December, 1954.

◄ Visit of Dimitris Svolopoulos, Director-General of Athens
Radio, to the BBC in April 1948. With Mr. Svolopoulos (fourth
from left) looking at the script for a programme broadcast in the
BBC Greek Service is George Angeloglou and members of the
Greek Section and studio staff.

Members of the BBC Greek Section who covered the Olympic Games for the BBC and Athens Radio, outside the BBC Broadcasting Centre, Wembley.
Left to right: George Megarefs, Stanley Mayers (deptuy Programme Organiser), Demetrios Manopoulos, Vrasidas Capernaros (with microphone), Mrs. S. Meehan, Anthony Mitsidis and Programme Organiser George Angeloglou.

CHAPTER 32

THE 1948 OLYMPIC GAMES HELD IN LONDON

1948 was a very eventful year. It saw the creation of Israel as an independent state, but to many parts of Greece it brought further misery and bloodshed - as the civil war was entering its final phase. To London it brought the first post-war Olympic Games, the 14th modern Olympiad - or the ration book games as we jokingly called them.

For the Greek Section, 1948 brought a new challenging and technologically exciting period in broadcasting with the first phase of our transmissions being rebroadcast by Athens Radio. This first post war Olympiad, staged so soon after almost five years of war, created tremendous difficulties and problems for both the host country and the athletic organisations of the world. London was still scarred by bomb damage, communications were still largely those of the early 1930s and there were still food and accommodation shortages. Money and luxuries were in short supply. It was the age of austerity. So for Britain to become the host to some

6,000 athletes from all over the world - Germany, Italy and Japan excepted - was a prodigious task. Britain hardly had a year in which to prepare for the Games, but the Labour Government and local authorities tackled the problems with determination and enthusiasm. The English, it is said, achieve more when they 've got their backs to the wall; so 1948 was all action stations. Wembley Stadium became the nerve centre of the Games. Richmond Park, Bedford College in Regents Park, and one or two RAF and Army camps became the homes of the 6,000 athletes. The Greek contingent consisting of 36 athletes was housed in Richmond Park. They were well accommodated. One or two of the Greeks complained that the park was too far from their training grounds, a few said that English food was quite colourless, but the majority loved the huge quiet green spaces of Richmond Park.

The Games were to begin on the 27th July. In the Greek Section we started preparing for the Games at the end of April. I had already gone to Athens for meetings with the D. G. of EIR, Nikos Svolopoulos, and his senior staff. In May Svolopoulos came to London and we decided that the Greek Section should carry the main reports of the Olympic Games and EIR would relay these reports in a special Olympic Report. For us, this was a great achievement because the daily relay would guarantee us a daily audience of at least a mil-

After the broadcast, members of the Section relax over a cup of coffee in the canteen.
Left to right: R. Inaraelo, Efrosini Sideropoulou, Stanley Mayes, Maria Bouka, Elli Megarefs

lion, plus the captive audience of the Greeks overseas in the USA, Egypt, other parts of Africa and in Asia, who totalled another million.

Elated by this great news, we all doubled our efforts to achieve best possible standards in sports commentaries. In agreement with EIR, we chose to broadcast every day a special Olympic bulletin of 15 minutes at 10 pm at night or 11 pm Greek time. This gave us the opportunity of pre-recording our running commentaries and of editing out mistakes or fluffs which were inevitable because our team, although consisting of excellent announcers, could not claim to be as good as the professional sports' commentators of the English services. Capernaros, Megarefs, Manolopoulos and Mitsidis became the announcers of the Olympic bulletins and were based at the Wembley Stadium. The rest of the Section remained in Bush House.

A few weeks later, the Greek Olympic team began to arrive; they would compete in the Marathon, the 5,000 metres, the pole vault, the javelin, rowing, shooting and in one or two of the wrestling events. One member of the Greek Section called Mylonas resigned in order to compete in the .22 rifle and pistol events in the Olympic Games. We met all the Greek athletes and did several interviews with them, and also with the Greek sports' commentators who came with the team.

To our great joy, the President of the British Olympic Committee was none other than Philip Noel Baker. Philip had been a former Olympic distance runner in 1912, 1920 and 1924. The 1920 Olympics were held in Antwerp, where Noel Baker was not only captain of the British team, but also won the silver medal in the 1,500 metres. He was a superb athlete, a gifted parliamentarian, devoted and tireless worker for peace and great lover of Greece. He spoke Greek quite well and he gave several talks in our service, always in Greek, with a slight trace of the Roumeli accent. During the London Olympics he was Secretary of State for Commonwealth Affairs and he gave the Inaugural speech. Philip, along with his wife and son were among some of our most distinguished 'outside contributors' to the Greek Section.

For me the most impressive and moving event of the 14th Olympiad was undoubtedly the first day of the Games when the 45 international teams paraded in front of King George VI after he had declared the Games open. The military bands then struck up a lively march and the 45 teams began to enter the Wembley arena.

The first flag to appear was the blue and white flag of Greece held by Stelios Kyriakidis, the Marathon champion of Greece, and followed by Ragazos, the other marathon runner and some 30 other Greek athletes. They wore smart light blue blazers - with the Greek flag and the five Olympic linked circles, emblazoned on the left-

hand pocket - a blue tie, grey trousers and white shoes.
The moment the Greek flag appeared, the whole stadium erupted in a thunderous applause and cries of
'zeto', mostly from the London Greek community, who
were there in full force. People rose to their feet as the
Greek flag passed in front of them and flowers were
thrown on the track. I had tears in my eyes as I heard
George Megarefs, who was doing a running commentary, pause for a moment to regain his composure. This
was the apotheosis of Greece; the small country, which
had never stopped fighting since the Italians invaded it
in October 1940. Poor, battered, exhausted Greece had
now come to represent the Greek spirit and athletic tra-
dition in the 14th modern Olympiad in London, when
only a few years ago she had been devastated by the German occupation, and was today still fighting a civil war.
The very idea that such a country and such people were
here in Wembley was enough to stir the hearts of
100,000 people who filled the Olympic Stadium.

The fact that, finally, the Greeks did not win a single
medal was only to be expected. After all we were com-
peting with countries like the U.S.A. Finland, Sweden
and Great Britain, countries which, for many years, had
developed organised sports structures, with national
coaches and some of whom had not experienced war or
occupation.

As for the marathon, which was now almost 2 kilometres longer than the race won by Spyridon Louis in 1896, did we expect Kyriakidis or Ragazos to win? Knowing the quality and training of many of the 41 marathon runners, it was a forlorn hope. On the 24th kilometre, Ragazos gave up with crippling cramps in his legs and an exhausted Kyriakidis bravely went on to finish 8th.

The actual finish of this marathon was quite sensational. A Belgian, Welshman and an Argentinian followed each other in that order into the Wembley Sta-

Stelios Kyriakidis, Megathlon champion of Greece, in Britain for the Olympic Games, broadcasting in the BBC Greek Service in July 1948.

dium. But the Belgian was completely exhausted and was overtaken by the Welshman, who in turn was overtaken by the strong Argentinian, Cabrera, who finally won the gold medal by a few yards from the Welshman!

Apart from our disappointment over the marathon, the London Olympic Games were otherwise a great tonic for us all. Although few Olympic records were broken in London, the 1948 Games produced some great personalities, not all of them American. The most colourful of these were one Czeck competitor and one Dutch woman athlete who won four gold medals. Zatopek was a long distance runner who charmed the crowds with his smiles and wise cracks, got the silver medal for 5,000 metres and the gold for 10,000 metres. In the next Olympic Games in 1951 in Helsinki, Zatopek won the marathon, the 5,000 and 10,000. He was a delight to see. The "Flying Woman", as she was called, was Fanny Blankers-Koen. She won the gold for 100 and 200 metres, the 80 metres hurdles and the 4 x 100 metres relay. She was the tops in London and people loved her.

The Olympic Games of 1948 were unforgettable; imbued as they were with the spirit and values which had inspired the 1896 revival of the Games. They also gave a great boost to British morale, which was later to be further enhanced by the 1951 Exhibition on the South Bank. For us, it boosted and sharpened our abilities in doing running commentaries and in working at speed to deadlines. We also learnt how to work with the Greek press and it certainly brought us in close touch with Athens Radio and its staff. In fact, after the Olympic Games, Athens Radio worked very closely with us and quite a few of its staff came to London to attend several of the BBC training courses. On the other hand, a senior radio engineer of ours, Bob Humphreys, was seconded to Athens Radio for a year, which later was extended to three years and finally to eight years!

I have a splendid and touching memento of the London Games. It is the Olympic badge that Stelios Kyriakidis wore on one of his two blazers. After the Games, he took it off the blazer and gave it to me saying "Mr George, we should like you and the Greek Section to have this badge as a token of our appreciation and thanks for the wonderful reception you gave to our Olympic team. Please frame it and hang it in your office." I certainly did that and today the famous badge, beautifully framed, hangs over my desk reminding me that the Greek Olympic spirit continues to inspire athletes all over the world.

CHAPTER 33

SIR COMPTON MACKENZIE

A delightful incident occurred in a restaurant in Soho. In the 1950's the restaurant was called "The Acropolis" - it doesn't exist today - and it was located at the junction of Percy Street and Charlotte Street. We were entertaining to dinner that genial philhellene and gifted writer, Compton Mackenzie. Compton had written a moving tribute to Greece to be broadcast in the Greek Service in celebration of the Ochi Day on the 28th October 1940. He came down from Scotland especially to record his talk. Almost every member of the Greek Section turned up in the studio to meet the famous man. His spoken Greek was very rusty, which was not bad considering that Compton had learnt his Greek during the First World War, as a British Intelligence Officer. But he enjoyed both the language and the lively atmosphere of the Greek Section. We had a good recording session in Bush House and at about 6.30 pm, together with four of my colleagues - Capernaros, Callinicos, Megarefs and Stanley Mayes my No. 2- we took Compton to dinner at The Acropolis.

The restaurant was not full, but Compton was soon recognised and people came up to shake him by the hand and ask for his autograph. He wanted to drink ouzo and his favourite wine, Retsina, and soon he was asking for Greek music as well. The proprietor obliged and the restaurant was then turned into a Greek taverna, but without the huge retsina barrels. Suddenly, half way through the meal, Mackenzie got up, got hold of a clean white serviette and without hesitating, he went to the dance floor and asked for a Kalamatianos. They put on a "Xekina mia Psaropoula". The lively rhythm immediately stirred everyone to beat time with their hands and feet. The whole place suddenly came alive and to my great surprise I saw Compton at the head of the chain waving the white serviette and performing rhythmic swirls with a display of colourful improvised steps. Mackenzie was again in his youth. The beat of the Kalamatianos had transformed him into the young man of 1910 when he first got to know Greece and chain dancing in Salonica. The pulsing beat of the Kalamatianos attracted more and more dancers on the floor, but always with Compton Mackenzie as the leader of the chain. Glasses* were broken on the dance floor and everyone was shouting "Bravo, Mackenzie, Na Mas Zessis Palika-

---

*The vulgar custom of breaking plates came in the 1960's, in fact after the film "Never on Sunday".

ri". When eventually the Kalamatianos stopped, we all sat down and Compton told us of Eleni, the Greek girl he had fallen in love with in Salonica in 1916. He then got up and made a speech. He had tears in his eyes and he was loudly applauded. After that, we all calmed down a bit, had some Greek sweets and a glass of Mavro-daphne to more joyful 'geia sas'.

It was then I noticed that Mackenzie was looking ti-red, very tired. Too much ouzo and Retsina I thought, and too much excitement for a man of his age. I becko-ned to one of the waiters saying, "please no more Retsi-na for Sir Compton, only strong coffee."

We gave him two large Greek coffees and soon it was 11 pm. His train to Edinburgh was leaving at 12 mid-night from Euston, so after exchanging emotional gree-tings, and the waiters getting all the autographs they wanted, we managed to get Compton out of the restau-rant and into a taxi with three of us, Capernaros, Calli-nicos and myself. We made Euston in good time, found Mackenzie's sleeping car and attendant, and got him on the train. The carriage was one of those modern sleepers with long corridors and windows you could pull down halfway. Compton stood in the corridor to say goodbye. I could see that he was very unsteady and that he held onto the window bar with both hands. At exactly mid-night the train began to move out slowly, and we fol-lowed it shouting "Kalo Taxidi" - Let's meet in Greece in the Summer. Abruptly, Compton took both hands off the bar that was steadying him and shouted in Greek, "Zito E Ellas". He had hardly finished the word ELLAS when he slipped to the ground and disappeared from view. I was alarmed, but Capernaros who was next to me said "He'll be alright, the attendants will look after him. He'll be in Edinburgh by the time he finishes his Zito."

We all laughed as we walked down the station platform. What a good way to see the great Scottish Philhellene go back to the Athens of the North. Naturally Compton Mackenzie would have preferred to be travelling to the real Athens and perhaps to meet again his first great love, Eleni!

Maria Callas broadcasting to Greece in November 1952.

CHAPTER 34

MARIA MENEGHINI CALLAS

The arrival of Maria Callas - Greeks also used her maiden name, Kalogeropoulou - in Bush House caused a great stir. It was the day after her triumph at Covent Garden in November 1952 where her performance in Bellini's Norma set new standards of excellence in both singing and acting. Callas had, in the last ten years of her international career, chosen Norma as her favourite role. Apart from the great music of Bellini, Norma's pride and passion blended perfectly with her temperament and character to produce a powerful performance on the Covent Garden stage.

Somehow, everyone in Bush House knew that she was coming to record an interview for the Greek Section, and for quite a while people stood at the entrance, and in the corridors, waiting to see Callas's arrival. She arrived in a large Daimler limousine accompanied, as usual, by her doting and possessive husband and agent, and her faithful secretary. Six of us met her. Two of us kissed her hand, while Meneghini kept a watchful eye on all these small intimacies.

George Megarefs, who was to do the interview, had already heard Callas sing as he was at the premiere the previous evening. We only had one ticket and I decided that it was best that George should be the lucky one. Anyway, he was not only a fine interviewer, but also an opera buff. He was absolutely ecstatic about the first night. He gave us a full account of all the important details and especially of the finale. "It was fantastic", he said, "to see Maria take curtain after curtain - twelve in all, one with the conductor and the others with the principals. Meantime the large stage had begun to look like a huge flowerbed of lilies, roses and carnations which had been thrown by the audience. Maria finally gave in to the thunderous applause and cheering and she sang an encore to the delirious delight of the huge audience, which by then had become more or less exhausted by their applauding, cheering and shouting, certainly more than Callas herself."

After everyone had met Maria and her husband, we went up to the VIP lounge for a cup of tea or coffee and then into the studio for the interview. Maria and Megarefs sat opposite each other at a large round table and her husband ensconced himself in between them. I had not noticed this quick move by Meneghini, so I dashed into the studio to talk to him. I explained politely that we never allowed non-participants to sit in the studio during a broadcast or recording. His reply was, "Excuse me, where Maria goes, I go. Maria and me, we are always together, I am her husband and also her agent". I suddenly realised we had a problem on our hands. The studio manager looked sombre. So I said, "Mr Meneghini, I know you love your wife very much, but this separation we are asking you to suffer is very short and it is for the good of your wife".

"The good of my wife, is to be with her marito. If not Maria will be sad and nervous" he replied as he grasped her hand firmly. I was going to say something nasty but instead I smiled and walked back into the control cubicle. My studio manager was on his feet. "The man is a pompous fool", he said, "so why argue with him and spoil the interview?

Let him sit in the studio at another table and I will position him so that Meneghini can look at Maria full face".

I went back to the studio and told the irate husband that the BBC, on this occasion, will make a supreme exception and allow him to sit in the studio but at another table, so as not to interfere with the ultra-sound waves! Fortunately Meneghini swallowed all this codswallop and went up to Maria, kissed her hand and told her that he was not abandoning her, but only moving to another table for the good of the recording. All this in Italian of course, delivered at high speed!

We moved Meneghini to another table and as I passed Maria, she whispered in Greek, "Take no notice of him, he gets a little mad when he becomes jealous. You see, too many Greeks" she smiled.

At last the interview started. Maria was very relaxed. She was happy to talk Greek and was delighted to tell the listeners about her success in London. She loved it all and she was proud that so many Greeks, including the Greek and Cypriot Ambassadors, had come to hear her. Now talking to Greece was even more moving she said.

Meneghini, meantime, sat rigidly at his table three metres away, never lifting his eyes from Maria and looking desperately unhappy because he could not hold her hand to give her encouragement. The moment she finished the interview, Meneghini got up and ran over to the microphone table and hugged and kissed Maria passionately, ignoring both me and the studio manager, who was trying to tell her about the quality of the recording. Maria said she thought the interview went well. Although she was very happy to hear herself talk Greek, she did not like her voice. I invited them to have tea or drinks, but Meneghini excused himself saying that Maria should have a rest at the hotel before the evening's performance. I think he really wanted to take her out of our grasp because he felt a complete outsider.

A little later the chauffeur driven Daimler called for them at the front entrance. Our parting was quite emotional. Maria was happily dispensing hugs and kisses to all the Greek Section, when suddenly Meneghini came up to me and began shaking my hand very warmly. "Mr Direttore", he said, "last night Maria was the supreme coloratura. This afternoon, she is also a beautiful Greek Goddess who spoke to Greece. Thank you BBC."

So after all, Giovanni Batista Meneghini was not only the jealous husband but also the star's agent and publicity organiser. A difficult double role, indeed!

CHAPTER 35

GENERAL CHRISTODOULOS
SVORONOS -TSIGANTES

During my years with the Greek Section I met a great many able men and women in various walks of life. Some were outstanding personalities; others were gifted interpreters and others were men of action.

I met and put on air many distinguished politicians and leaders of the time - Greek, British and French. One who made a very great impression on me - and who influenced me - was General Christodoulos Svoronos - Tsigantes, known to his friends as Lakis.

Although several times in his life he had flirted with the idea of becoming a politician somehow he always remained faithful to his army career. But as an ardent Venizelist, and a staunch Republican, he took part in several coups d'etat. The most important was that of March 1935. The coup, which was inspired by his old mentor General Plastiras, had tragic consequences not only for the liberal high-spirited officers who took part

212

but also for Venizelos and the Republic. General Kondylis, the Minister of War crushed the Republican coup, and severe sentences were passed on the rebels.

Among the middle ranking officers were Tsigantes and his brother John. They were sentenced to life imprisonment, but the sentence was later commuted and they were cashiered from the army. This was a humiliation Tsigantes never forgot. "What do you expect from generals of the calibre of Kondylis? Republican one day, king-maker the next!" he said with his typical humorous understatement. Tsigantis was always undramatic in speech, always understating any situation. I never heard him abuse an opponent; instead he would make a wry remark and deliver it with a smile and a twinkle in his eye - more effective than any abusive comment.

But if he was circumspect and diplomatic in his utterances he was anything but cautious with his life. He loved excitement and adventure. He once told me, "men become old before their time if they forget to live dangerously, they become lax and lazy and lose all ambition. You must love life like you love a woman - with fire and passion. When nothing excites you any more, you are dead!" This was typical of him and his life - which was one risky incident after another - with him always the adventurer.

In 1936, when Metaxas finally established his dictatorship, Tsigantes was ordered to leave Greece. He

General Tsigantes - Director General of EIR.

214

went back to the country of his youth, Romania. His brother John went with him, but they didn't stay there for long. They joined the Foreign Legion and saw action in Abyssinia. Then war came, France fell, and they joined the Free French army and went to fight in Africa. John was later killed in 1942 fighting the Italians in Athens.

In 1942 Tsigantes, with a group of fellow officers, formed the Sacred Battalion. He became its Commanding Officer and the Battalion fought at El Alamein under Montgomery. After the Germans were defeated in North Africa Tsigantes went on to form a commando unit and operated in the German occupied Aegean. When Italy capitulated in 1943 he was sent by GHQ Cairo to occupy Samos and prevent the Germans from taking the island. Tsigantes descended on the Samiots like a deus ex machina - by parachute. It was typical of the man that he had never made a parachute drop before.

"They showed me how to put the thing on," he said," and I spent an afternoon watching a few men doing jumps. That's all - nothing to it."

"But you didn't do a trial jump?" I asked.

"One drop is enough for me. If I break a leg - too bad. Why tempt fate twice?" he laughed.

In fact the parachute drop on Samos was a great success. He didn't break a leg, but got tangled up in a prickly pear, quite near our family house.

"The rest was a piece of cake," he said. "The Italians

were demoralised and soon surrendered. They were expecting the Germans and when they realised we were Greek commandos they were relieved. As the Italian commander handed me his pistol he said he was pleased to surrender to the brave and civilised Greeks. I knew what he meant."

When the war in Greece came to an end Tsigantes sought new challenges. In 1945 he was made Military Governor of the Aegean and then Military Governor of the Dodecanese until 1948, when he became Governor of Euboea. Then, as a Major General, he decided to retire from the Army and became a military and political commentator for various newspapers. At this time he seriously thought of entering politics as a Liberal candidate - but he failed to get a seat in the 1950 elections.

His big challenge came in 1950 when he was appointed Director-General of EIR, the National Radio Organisation. It was during this period that I really got to know him well. He often came to London and met many of the senior executives of the BBC, including the then Director-General, Sir Ian Jacob. Tsigantes recognised the power and influence of the BBC and wanted to model EIR on the Corporation. The BBC gave Tsigantes the fullest co-operation, and seconded Bob Humphreys, one of its senior engineers as Technical Adviser to work with him. With Tsigantes at the helm EIR underwent many changes to take it into a more enlightened period of broadcasting, with the calibre and quality of its programmes reflecting the vision and lightness of touch, as well as the courage, of its Director-General.

When I visited him in Athens he always had exciting ideas for programmes for the Greek Section as well as suggestions for the BBC English Services. He asked me to bring other members of the BBC with me on my yearly visits to Athens in order to have a constant exchange of views and ideas between the two organisations. One such person was Lawrence Gilliam, Head of Features of the BBC Domestic Services. Gilliam, I and a number of talented Greek writers and actors recorded two one hour programmes in Greece. These were broadcast with great success on the BBC Home and Overseas Services. Tsigantes also cultivated close relations and co-operation with the Americans and French with the result that EIR acquired a great deal of modern technical equipment.

I remember one occasion in August 1951 when Tsigantes invited Richard Erstein, my opposite number in the Voice of America, to meet me in Athens. I had always wanted to meet the Head of the American Greek Service and now Tsigantes made this possible. As Laurence Gilliam, was also in Athens at the time, the General decided to give a big dinner to mark the meeting of the Heads of the Greek Sections. With his flair for the unusual Tsigantes gave the dinner, not in a big hotel, but under the huge pylon of the main Athens Radio transmitter at Liossia. It was a memorable occasion, attended by many well-known Greek and foreign personalities - among them was Sir Brooks Richard, then head of the Information Department of the British Embassy and later to be British Ambassador in Athens. The photographs from that dinner show Tsigantes in a relaxed mood, contented and fulfilled in his post as Director General of EIR, a position he held until 1953. Then he resigned out of sheer stubbornness because he could not work under Papagos when he became Prime Minister, in spite of the latter's efforts to persuade him to stay on.

But apart from functions like this it was travelling around the country with Tsigantes that was most rewarding. Driven by his faithful ex-sergeant chauffeur we went to meet ordinary people to talk about the impact of the BBC's Greek broadcasts. Everywhere we went he was greeted as a war hero, mobbed by local officials and the general public alike. What a wonderful job he did for Greek Radio. He would have made a superb ambassador for Greece. Alas, the politicians did not appreciate his talents as a diplomat and negotiator and he was never offered a diplomatic post.

One particular trip we made in the Peloponnese stays in my mind. We went together with Charles Crutchfield, who was vice-president of one of the American Television and Radio Networks. We stayed near Kalavryta at the lovely country house of Zaimis, surrounded by views of lush rolling hills and vineyards. During the days our party of five travelled by jeep all over the area around Kalavryta. We visited the mass grave of the men of the town who were massacred by the Germans in 1941 as a reprisal for the defiance of the Greek Resistance in the area. It was a moving moment when the General spoke with great compassion to the black dressed mothers and widows of the executed men, who kissed his hands and embraced him with tears in their eyes.

Then at night we would sit out under the whispering pines over dinner and coffee under a yellow moon. Crutchfield played chess with one of the ladies in the party, while I played cards with the General. We played that Russian card game Sixty Six, which Tsigantes played with his customary daring; but he was a gambler and he often lost. One night I had the luck of the devil and won almost every game we played. In the end the General gave up in disgust. "It's a good thing" he said "that you are not Catherine The Great. Just imagine how many heads would have rolled in the morning." He was referring to one of his favourite stories, which told how Catherine The Great loved to play Sixty Six with her lovers, especially ones she had tired of. "If he won" said Tsigantes, "he made love to her. If he lost he was shot at dawn. And generally the Empress won. Goodnight!"

During my travels on official visits with the General we covered the Peloponnese and went to Volos, Salonica and the Aegean islands. Particularly memorable was the trip to Hydra where we visited the beautiful Koundouriotis house - and met old Mrs Koundouriotis - and then to the house and estate of Stamatis Voudouris where we spent a few days. This, of course, was before Jules Dassin shot Phaedra in that location with Melina Mercouri, Anthony Perkins and the notorious Aston Martin - the only sports car that ever got to Hydra and for which a special road had to be built.

Wherever we went Tsigantes was treated like a film star. As one villager said to me, "You must be happy to walk beside a man like the General. There are not many like him in the world." I was proud and happy to be a friend of Tsigantes and to have travelled with him during his few moments of leisure and relaxation. To me he was an extraordinary person combining as he did the qualities of dynamic action with those of an urbane and cultured mind and the quick wit of a born conversationalist. He was dignified and proud but never aloof; philosophical and diplomatic yet stubborn in support of his moral principles. He was tough and courageous, yet he could be gentle, romantic, and at times very sentimental. He always appeared positive and optimistic, but if the reverse was ever the case he never showed it.

CHAPTER 36

ALKIS ANGELOGLOU

One day in 1953, I received a letter from Greece which disturbed me. It was written by Alkis Angeloglou, a cousin of mine - a second cousin on my father's side who was gradually achieving a reputation as one of the new young writers of Greece. He wrote that he was in dire financial straits, and wanted to leave Greece, and was asking for some help from me in the shape of employment in the Greek Section. I feared that such a request was bound to come some time soon but I also knew that it would not be difficult to refuse - because my cousin had very little English.

All news had to be translated into Greek, and I reckoned that my cousin would require, at the very least, three to four months of intensive study. I was fully aware that as Head of the Greek Section, I had to show no partiality towards my cousin. He certainly had the ability to become a translator-announcer but it was a question of time - and he would have to pass the standard test to which every new member of the Greek Section submitted.

In due course he arrived in London to take the test. He got a C. The examiner who tested him sent me a report which stated that Alkis could get a B+ (the mark required) in another two or three months. We decided to give him another chance, but in the meantime he had to practise translations every day.

He turned up on the appointed date looking cheerful as if he was to slay the fearful monster at last. In fact this time he went into the examination hall at running pace and had the complete translation and microphone test. He came out of the examination laughing. He had at last killed the dragon! He gained a B+. The whole Section was on his side. Everyone shook him by the hand, and wished him success. He was now a member of the Greek Section. No-one was more happy than I - there were now two Angeloglous in the Greek Section.

Alkis was very pleased both with himself, and with the English language. He went to Athens to settle his affairs. In the meantime his wife - who was a graduate in Greek literature with Athens University - had successfully applied for the position of Head of Foreign Correspondence in a large Greek shipping firm in the City of London. So, with two incomes, life in London for the Angeloglou family was now much easier.

I congratulated him and I told him that now he was going to try to make a name for himself in English. He smiled and promised to fulfil this ambition. My faith in

Alkis was justified and he became a fine broadcaster. His admiration for things British knew almost no bounds. Yet his idiosyncratic, stoical and courteous manner masked the considerable courage of his convictions.

Unfortunate events led to Alkis' dismissal from the Greek Section on the orders of the BBC hierarchy in September 1955. During the Cyprus crisis, in mid-September - Alkis happened to be on duty. For his Press Review that day he had chosen relevant extracts from the British press and included a detailed dispatch from Noel Barber in the Daily Mail of September 14th. This covered the looting and burning of Greek shops and houses in Istanbul. Barber reported how Turkish Cypriot extremists, stirred up by anti-Greek elements in Turkey had set fire to every Greek, Armenian and Jewish shop and provision store in Istanbul's main street, the famous Avenue of Independence. In the fires that followed many died, including a number of Greek priests. Demonstrations had prevented the fire brigade putting out the fires so some buildings burned for thirty-six hours.

On his way to the studio Alkis was told that a directive, just received from the Colonial Office, directed that the Barber dispatch should not be included in his broadcast. Alkis viewed that the directive was a negation of what he saw as a basic freedom. He said clearly that it was his duty to read the dispatch. He was duly warned of the consequences, but he read the dispatch and was sacked immediately.

▲ *Irene Pappas, the Greek film actress, is interviewed during a visit to England by Vrasidas Capernaros of the BBC Greek Service for the weekly magazine programme "Radio Chronicles".*

Gina Bachaeur, the distinguished pianist, gave a recital for the BBC Greek Service in June 1948. With her in the studio are, <u>left to right:</u> *Vrasidas Capernaros, George Angeloglou, conductor Alec Sherman and Stanley Mayes.* ▼

After leaving the Greek Section he went to Greece and for a time worked at the Ministry to the Prime Minister. However, his love of England brought him back to London in 1957 where he joined the Press Office of the Greek Embassy, where he stayed for the next ten years. When the Colonels established their dictatorship in 1967 Alkis resigned within a week, telling the Ambassador, in his typically outspoken way, that it was his duty to close the doors of the Embassy and fly the Greek flag at half-mast.

Unable to stay idle for long, Alkis returned to the Greek Section in Bush House - where the past was quickly forgiven and forgotten - and he accepted the post of Commentator. He was soon back on form happily broadcasting again to Greece with his characteristically informative and entertaining talks on the British literary scene - and writing articles for Athens newspapers and literary magazines.

He retired from the BBC in 1975.

CHAPTER 37

CYPRUS V BRITAIN   1940-41 and 1954-57

always feared that some time later in the war, or soon after, Britain would seriously clash with Greece over the question of Cyprus. Although the Greeks admired Britain, they could not accept that an island inhabited mostly by Greeks, and whose history was part of the history of ancient Greece, should be held as a vassal by a foreign power.

Of course we in the Greek Section had to accept the status quo imposed on us by Britain, but deep down in our Greek psyche there were many reservations which surfaced every now and then and caused quite a few anxieties and difficulties in broadcasting. We had to bear in mind that the policies of the Foreign Office were not always the same as those of the Colonial Office. After a while it became apparent that it was not practical or intelligent to talk to the Cypriots in the same manner as the rest of our audience, especially those living in Africa or Australia.

In late 1940 Cyprus sent a small force of volunteers

Morning conference of the Greek Section when staff discuss transmissions for the day. <u>*Left to right:*</u> *Stanley Mayes, George Angeloglou, Frosso Sideropoulou, Alkis Angeloglou, M. Crispis and Vrasidas Capernaros.*

to Egypt to help in the desert transportation of the 8th Army. They brought a troop of mules from Cyprus; the mule is a tough animal capable of carrying heavy loads over rough ground although inevitably jeeps and lorries finally replaced the mules.

We did not pay particular attention to this event, which caused considerable anxiety at the Colonial Office who pointed out that we hardly ever covered the important events that happened on this beautiful and very English island. I made the point that after all the war was our main focus, but the Colonial Office thought that we were missing opportunities with regard to Cyprus.

When we discussed this at our daily meetings the ma-

The Rt. Hon. Philip Noel-Baker, M. P., who broadcast a personal tribute in the BBC Greek Service in July, 1953, on the occasion of the death of General Nicholas Plastiras, former Prime Minister of Greece.

jority thought that such coverage was more appropriate in English transmissions directed to a wider imperial audience. When this was reported back to the Colonial Office they decided that I should have a meeting with one of its Assistant Secretaries to clarify the situation - that the Greek Section seemed to have little interest in Cyprus except when Cyprus was in the news. At the same time a strange reaction to Cyprus started to worry us. A number of my staff became aware of the Cypriot accent and were not in favour of having Cypriot announcers.

This prejudice was quite common in those early days among the London Greeks, but we managed to counter it by starting a special daily broadcast for Cyprus. We were lucky because, at this time, Michael Cacoyannis arrived in London to study law and we thought that he would become an excellent announcer. Michael was the son of the eminent and politically active lawyer, Sir Panayiotis Cacoyannis, who had been knighted during the short reign of Edward VIII. At the same time Beba Clerides, the sister of Glafkos Clerides, was in London studying. She also came from a distinguished Limassol family, and her brother, Glafkos, after a long and brilliant political career, became President of the Cyprus Republic. Michael was appointed to run the small Cypriot Section, with Beba as his number two.

After much argument the BBC accepted that we would have to have separate transmissions devoted to the needs and interests of our Cypriot listeners who numbered well over 250,000, including of course the Turkish minority, who were also served by the BBC Turkish broadcasts. Two people made the division possible thanks to their understanding of the delicate issues involved - David Ashby and Michael Cacoyannis. For me the separation of the Greek and Cypriot Sections was a blessing because in this way the Greek Section avoided getting embroiled in the Cypriot issues, which did not really interest the majority of our listeners. We also avoided the stupid accusation that our broadcasts were spoken in a parochial Cypriot accent instead of the pure Athenian accent - which was not really the case.

So within a couple of weeks we had a fully-fledged Cypriot Section broadcasting a daily bulletin to Cyprus. In due course this section became part of the Overseas Services and was based in another building at 200 Oxford Street. I suggested that Michael should be independent of me. In fact we managed to have completely independent transmissions. It was a great success and very soon, thanks to the common understanding between Michael and myself, apart from news and the added flavour of the Cypriot accent, the Cypriot broadcast, which preceded our evening transmission, was almost the same as ours. Everybody was satisfied and the two broadcasts continued to duplicate each other with great success.

But years later, and under completely different circumstances, it was Cyprus again that caused the big storm in the Greek section which culminated in the destruction of the Greek Section that we had created over the years.

The Cyprus struggle, which started in 1954, severely strained Anglo-Greek friendship. The Foreign Office demanded that we adopt an aggressive attitude towards Greece, as a counter to the anti-British propaganda of E.I.R. With the full backing of my staff, I refused to comply. "It was foolish and short-sighted", I argued, "to destroy the great popularity of the Greek Section for the sake of political expediency." "Cyprus," I continued, "would sooner or later be given her independence and Archbishop Makarios would kiss the Queen's hand, but meantime the BBC's Greek Section would be savaged by the Greek press and radio." My argument was not accepted and the pressure on me increased. By 1957 every present member of the Greek Section had resigned and finally I too went down with the sinking ship - or to be more precise I was thrown overboard to the sharks.

I left the Greek Section in 1957, but continued my BBC career in the television service and later as a producer of talks and current affairs programmes for Radios 3 and 4 in the domestic service.

CHAPTER 38

FINALE

LOOKING BACK OVER TWENTY YEARS OF BROADCASTING TO GREECE

This is a transcript of a talk I gave in Greek on 2nd January 1959

Twenty years have gone by since that unforgettable evening of the 28th September in 1939 when "E-DO LONDINO" was first heard over the ether. A life full of hard work, full of continuous hopes and disappointments. A life devoted to duty, but also to the idea of liberty and to honest and impartial journalism. It is difficult for me - who had the honour to start the Greek Section and to guide it for so many years - to select and recall now the events that were momentous at the time. At any rate, the most important chapters in the history of the Greek Section were also of equal concern to all its listeners.

In the first phase of the war we were so to speak the

apostles of the ideal of democracy. In the war in Albania we heartened, applauded and extolled the triumphs of the Greek army. In the black years of the Italian/-German occupation, we were the forbidden voice of consolation and encouragement. And later, we reported the war in the desert, El Alamein and the final defeat of Hitler on the second front. Then followed the sad and tragic events of the civil war in Greece.

In every one of these vital chapters the Greek Section played its role. Each one of these phases of the war made special demands on us, brought new difficulties, created problems and eventual solutions.

The Greeks of the Greek Section were equal to the great demands made upon them because they had the burning will of the volunteer, of the apostle. To have been a member of the Greek Section in those days meant that you had to be a member of a fighting fraternity, which you joined because you believed in its aims and philosophy. That was the spirit that attracted so many young Greeks to come and work in the Greek Section and to learn something of its methods, traditions and principles. They came from all parts of Greece as well as from the large Greek communities in Egypt, Turkey and America. More than two hundred Greeks went through the Greek Section during these twenty years of our history. They all brought with them their enthusiasm and personal abilities. And when they left they took with them something of the traditions we tried to develop: co-operation, brotherhood, devotion to the truth and the tireless pursuit of improvement.

For this reason, and with some personal pride and with great emotion, I would like to end my talk tonight, and after so many years, by sending warm brotherly greetings to all the young men and women who created this great family of the Greek Section and who are now scattered in every corner of the earth. I send my warmest wishes to you all.

FOOTNOTE

I would like to put on record my disappointment that, at the end of the war, for various political reasons, the then Greek Government never officially acknowledged the war service of those who served in the BBC's Greek Section. If you go into the Council Chamber in Broadcasting House you will see plaques acknowledging the service of many war-time sections, like that of the Belgian, Danish, Dutch and French governments - and even one from the President of the United States of America. But there is not even an official letter from the government of Greece. Not a word to thank all those who performed such valuable service for the allied war effort and for the cause of Greece. I never understood this omission. But I always remember the cynical words of Demetrios Caclamanos who said to me: " To be acknowledged by the Greeks, you've got to be dead - and even then you will be damned lucky!"

For the record here is a list, in alphabetical order, of all those members of the Greek Section who served during the years 1939 - 1957. The dates indicate when each person joined the BBC. Unfortunately, some of the BBC records have been destroyed and I apologise for any omissions or inaccuracies.

Founder members of the Greek Section
on 28th September 1939

George Angeloglou
Sotiris Soteriadis
Basil Constantinidis
Constantine Gregoriadis
Anthony Mitsidis
Mary Moschona

Members of the Greek Section 1939-1957

Angelos Abelas	1950
Lefteris Adam	1950
Alkis Angeloglou	1953
Spyros Babouris	1953
Jenny Bailey	1953
Panos Bakirtzis	1941
Angeliki Bennet	1946
Maria Bouka	1949
Panos Callinicos	1941
Vrasidas Capernaros	1941
Michael (Mihalis) Cacoyannis	1940
Beba Cleridou	1941
Nicos Coccalis	1953
Nicos Constantinidis	1947
Dionissios (Nionios) Damiris	1940
Stelios Democratis	1941
V. Dracoulis	1941
Demetrios Fildissakos	1953

Costas Hadjiargyris	1941
Haris Haralambopoulos	1952
Kali Jenks	1940
Costas Krassas	1952
Popy Krassa	1952
Nicos Krassas	1953
Kakos Kyriakidis	1941
Zissimos Lorentzatos	1953
John Leatham	1956
Demetrios Manolopoulos	1941
Petros Marsellos	1942
Gordon Mate	1942
Stanley Mayes	1947
George Megarefs	1946
Elli Megarefs	1949
George Mitsidis	1942
Costas Mylonas	1945
Irene Pandelidou	1943
George Pastelidis	1948
Alecos Papamarkou	1952
Noel Paton	1942
Irene Poulopoulou	1941
Thrasyvoulos Raptopoulos	1941
Helen Raptopoulou	1941
Phyllis Reekie	1942
Apostolos Sahinis	1954
Frosso Sideropoulou	1942
Aristotelis Sismanidis	1941
Costas Sismanis	1957
Dimitrios Soulidis	1953

Fethros Stassinos	1947
Mihalis Stylianou	1953
Hector Tembros	1942
Neokosmos Tzallas	1955
Nanos Valaoritis	1948
Byron Veinoglou	1942
Mrs Veinoglou	1942
Georgina Wood	1941